1 00

THE ESSENTIALS OF
HORSEMANSHIP

(*W. W. Rouch & Co*)

LT.-COLONEL HARRY LLEWELLYN, O.B.E., ON FOXHUNTER

THE ESSENTIALS OF HORSEMANSHIP

by Brigadier General

J. F. Lamont

C.B., C.M.G., D.S.O.

(late R.H. and F.A.)

CONSTABLE · LONDON

LONDON

PUBLISHED BY

Constable and Company Ltd

10–12 ORANGE STREET W.C.2

INDIA

Orient Longmans Ltd

BOMBAY   CALCUTTA   MADRAS

CANADA

Longmans, Green and Company

TORONTO

SOUTH *and* EAST AFRICA

Longmans, Green and Company Ltd

CAPETOWN   NAIROBI

AUSTRALIA

Walter Standish and Sons

SYDNEY

First published 1955

PRINTED IN GREAT BRITAIN BY
EBENEZER BAYLIS AND SON LTD., THE
TRINITY PRESS, WORCESTER, AND LONDON

CONTENTS

ACKNOWLEDGMENT

Chapter XI of this book originally appeared in *Riding*. The author expresses his gratitude for permission to reproduce it.

LIST OF ILLUSTRATIONS

7

NOTE ON THE FRONTISPIECE

Lt.-Colonel Harry Llewellyn, o.b.e.

It is indeed a privilege to have been granted permission to reproduce this photograph. It portrays a superlative sportsman who possesses in a marked degree all the essentials of horsemanship and a man who has been universally proclaimed the Show Jumping Champion of the World. Not only has he proved himself in Horse Shows and Olympic Games, but he has finished second and fourth in the Grand National and has won the Foxhunters' Steeplechase at Cheltenham, together with innumerable lesser Chases and Point-to-Points. By his inspiration, planning and example he has steered the British Team to the First Place in practically all the international competitions. Every rider who wishes to become a horseman should regard Colonel Llewellyn as the *beau ideal* who, moreover, is a Master of Hounds and a grand man over a country.

In conclusion, mention must be made of Foxhunter, that gallant, generous old horse, who, as a consistent performer, is justly famous. When Colonel Llewellyn and Foxhunter enter the Ring the spontaneous outburst of applause proclaims the well-merited popularity of both.

J.L.

9

PREFACE

FRIENDS have persuaded me to put into writing a life-long experience of the practical and theoretical sides of the art of Horsemanship.

Race-riding, training, polo, hunting, hacking, breaking and making, combined with the every-day life of a Horse Gunner, taught me much in the practical, while teaching, lecturing and reading much in the theoretical side.

No matter what form of employment or recreation one may take up, it is, or should be, essential to study well its theory and practice. Theory by itself is not sufficient. Practice by itself, will get one further, but not all the way. It is a judicious mixture of theory and practice, that will bring one out on top.

It was long the habit of horsemen to scoff at anything in the nature of book learning and theory. "You can't learn to ride out of a book," the old-timers used to say. No more you can, but you can learn a great deal, absorb good advice and get all sorts of useful tips, which, put into practice, make for proficiency.

My advice to riders, is to read as many books as possible, subscribe to or have access to those magazines and weeklies, which deal with Horses and Horsemanship and provide good photographs, even fiction is often instructive as well as entertaining.

11

Although a good deal of repetition is inevitable some new tips, hints, or suggestions are almost sure to be met with which will prove helpful and beneficial.

In this treatise my endeavour has been to produce something that will prove of assistance to riders of all stages, and to provide food for thought for Instructors and even for the old hands who have "ridden all my life". A good portion is devoted to the elementary stages, for all structures must be built on a thorough foundation; in riding this is of the utmost importance. Bad habits acquired by beginners are difficult to eradicate, but it can be done. If a rider will recognize that he or she is at fault in any particular, it is necessary to set to work to eliminate such shortcomings, due undoubtedly to faulty instruction at the beginning. The perusal of these pages may throw light on some hitherto unsolved problem, difficulty or defect; it will be for the reader to put the solution or cure into careful practice.

Many years as an instructor has convinced me that the method best calculated to produce the most satisfactory results is to put to the pupils the proven facts, the outstanding examples, the fundamental principles, the why and the wherefore and the for and the against, after which the pupil must think it out for himself, think it all over and put the theory into practice.

The pupil must not, after the lesson is over, never give it all a thought until the next time. No matter how long one is at it, one can always be learning. Those who never progress are those who won't be taught.

When I joined the service and was at the 'Shop',* the military system of instruction was, I fear, not on sound lines. In those days we had no Weedon nor Saugor. During leave I spent a good deal of time in France and Germany, where I learnt much from Civilian Instructors, who were masters of the Haute Ecole. For the rest I had to get down to it on my own, watching and endeavouring to copy the fine horsemen I saw and met. Books also assisted me considerably; self-education gives one a more understanding insight into the difficulties encountered by others, particularly by the novices, and forces one to work out cause and effect.

What I aim at in this treatise is to assist a rider to climb up on any reasonably broken horse. Make it do whatever he may require of it, never spoil its mouth or manners, in fact if anything improve it in these particulars. Thus he will thoroughly enjoy a ride and help the horse to enjoy it too. I hope to help the learner to sit well over fences and eventually to perform in the ring, at point-to-points and even at steeplechasing and polo. Dressage or the Haute Ecole is another story and should only be taken up as a study after the student has become a thoroughly efficient horseman, in the stages I am dealing with. The pupil must have attained great proficiency before attempting Breaking, Making and

* Royal Military Academy, Woolwich.

Re-Breaking, another distinct branch of the Art of Horsemanship.

Riding has become a National Recreation, a most desirable state of affairs. Time was when only those people rode who were amply moneyed and leisured or who had to use the horse as a conveyance. Such took to riding naturally, being taught by their parents' grooms or coachmen. To-day it is not so, therefore there is a very definite need for efficient instruction both practical and theoretical.

The illustrations are entirely photographic, for the reason that they demonstrate the true happenings of things more faithfully than do drawings or sketches. Without appearing in any way invidious in my choice, I have selected as examples subjects who have proved themselves in competition to be at the top of the tree and therefore admirable examples to follow. There may be many as good, but personally I know of none better. The utmost benefit can be derived from a close study of these photographs. One's resolve should be: "What they can do, so also can I." Aim high, aim for perfection: even if you do not attain it, you will get somewhere near. Whereas if you do not aim high you will get nowhere. I have not attempted to deal with the side saddle as a seat. However, all the points dealt with are applicable to both side and astride.

Before discussing the subjects to be dealt with in this book it may be advisable to examine the mental and physical attributes necessary for those who aim to acquire proficiency in Equitation. To some these essentials may at first sight appear unattainable; this is not so. Anyone who really takes careful stock of his or her natural propensities can definitely develop the necessary attributes, or even create them where deficiencies are recognized, and thus attain the required standard.

It is often said that you must start young to be any good; this is quite wrong. In my long life I have known a number of people who started fairly late who became absolutely first class, and even quite elderly people who rode sufficiently well to thoroughly enjoy their riding. Moreover, it is fallacious to say that some aren't the shape for it and will never be able to ride. Of course a long leg and a flat thigh are a help, but I have known riders with short legs and round thighs who were first class in the saddle, so pay no heed to that kind of criticism.

As in the case of physical development, so with mental or nervous inadequacy. A limb or muscle by judicious exercises can be worked up to meet any reasonable demands. Equally, those mental or subconscious shortcomings can be rectified, but we must, by the exercises of self-analysis and will power, put matters right by our own exertion, aided perhaps by friendly and sympathetic assistance. This is where a really good Instructor comes in.

Some readers at this stage may object that they have no wish to perform at the White City nor to go Hunting or Steeplechasing. All they want is to be able to enjoy a quiet hack. The answer to that objection is that the principle remains the same, whatever you may be doing on a horse, and an indifferent rider, even when quietly hacking, is a potential danger to himself and his mount. Moreover the better we ride, the more we appreciate the rhythm and motion of a well balanced horse.

I sincerely trust that this book will prove useful, give food for thought and enable all those who ride to grasp the essentials which will make riding come more easily to the beginner and create increased interest to those who are more experienced.

CHAPTER I

ESSENTIAL ATTRIBUTES

The First Essential is Courage. Many books
have been written about courage, but it remains
hard to define: it is the sustaining factor which
enables one, faced with danger, to get on with the
job in a calm and collected manner. The whole
secret of eliminating fear in riding is to ask oneself,
"Of what am I afraid?" One will find, perhaps to
one's surprise, that the risks of a fall and those
attendant upon a fall are considerably less than
those arising from excessive eating or drinking, or
in crossing the road.

Nerve. What is called *nerve* is perhaps another
way of describing courage, but to many it means
absence of nervousness, which, no matter how
highly-strung one may be, is a matter of will-power.
In my experience, many nervous riders have become cool, courageous horsemen by the exercise of
will-power. By banishing anticipation they gained
confidence, thereby greatly improving their horsemanship. If confident, one can concentrate, if one
concentrates one improves.

Health has a good deal to do with nerve. Riding

17   B

makes for health. Riding requires nerve, but at the same time begets nerve. An old jump trainer once said to me, "Riding and drinking are two men's jobs."

Even Temper is essential. Petulant, irritable, bad-tempered people will never ride well. Experience has proved that irritability and bad temper are often the outward sign of inward funk. Therefore control your temper, it will be a great help in controlling your horse.

Resolution. The determination to attain perfection should always be in the learner's mind. Do not blame the horse if he goes badly for you, and should you see him go smoothly for another, try to discover where *you* have failed. If there is a knowledgeable person present, do not be too proud to ask where you have gone wrong, although in some riding schools, I fear, that would be like the blind leading the blind. One of your resolutions must be to make the horse do your bidding without using violence. A horse coming at a fence half-heartedly can be made to take it by a determined horseman, where a weak or nervous rider will fail. Throw your heart over first, then ride him at it. This trite and hackneyed phrase crystallizes a wealth of wisdom and experience.

Patience is another essential. Patience when learning. You can't negotiate Aintree after twelve lessons. Patience with the horse. He is not the most intelligent of animals, but he is a creature of habit and has a long memory and is generally anxious to please. He must be given to understand what you want, while you must have the patience, firstly to learn how to handle him, then to get him to do what you want. "Be to his virtues ever kind and to his faults a little blind."

Quick Thinking is a further essential. As the riding improves so will the mind work more quickly. If you are naturally quick you will learn more rapidly. If you are slow, as your horsemanship improves, so will your mental reactions gain speed. You must think more quickly than the horse, in fact anticipate what he is going to do before he does it or even before he thinks about it. A senior officer, an indifferent horseman, was out hacking in the Long Valley, when a loquacious subaltern overtook him and began to chatter. "Damn it," said the senior officer, "don't talk to me, can't you see I am busy riding?" Never be busy riding, at the same time never be caught off your guard.

An Active Body is important to the potential horseman. The more trained and flexible the muscles, the more easily will a good seat and all that that implies be attained. With muscles hard and fit, a toss is nothing to worry about. Riding in itself hardens the muscles and prevents the waistline from obtruding itself.

Sensitivity, by which I mean an acute sensitiveness, is a further attribute to good horsemanship. This quality helps the rider to understand the horse he is riding at the moment, to feel exactly what is required in the way of aids, rein pressure and so on. Hands, seat and legs must be sensitive. The sensitive mind will promote a sympathy and understanding which will give confidence to any horse, and particularly so in training, handling and breaking a young one.

The beginner will not find this sensitivity ready made, but it will come as he attains seat and hands. Naturally, the more sensitive one is by nature, the easier it is to get on terms with one's horse.

The naturally brutal and domineering person, in other words the born bully, will never get horses to go kindly unless and until he has mastered himself.

There is a lot of bad horsemanship to be seen. The pity of it is, the majority are firmly convinced that they can ride.

Assuming that one has the above natural virtues, if I may so call them, or that one is at least anxious to cultivate and acquire them, let us then take the next step.

CHAPTER II

THE SEAT

A FIRM and balanced seat is the initial essential to proficiency. It is a combination of grip and balance. On no matter do the experts differ more than on the relative importance of grip and balance, some affirming that they should be fifty-fifty, others insisting that it should be a fourth grip to three-quarter balance, others again putting it the other way round. Let us forget theory and go all out to acquire these two *desiderata* to the utmost.

Grip. This is a muscular effort, depending on the aductors, better known as the tailor or riding muscles, which are hardly ever used, except in riding, figure skating, ski-ing, cross kicking at football and by a tailor sitting cross-legged. A tyro therefore finds that his grip is feeble and that the aductors soon tire.

Beginners are strongly advised to go through a course of P.T., specializing in building up the aductors, back and stomach muscles. The benefits of such exercises are incalculable. Not only does grip come sooner, but the risk of what is called "Riders' Strain" is reduced to a minimum. In fact all, beginners or not, who only ride occasionally are strongly recommended to make a daily habit of these exercises.

Balance is the adjustment of the rider's weight in accordance with the horse's movements, thus assisting the grip as much as possible. Let us try to illustrate this definition. Suppose the horse swerves or turns to the right? Unless the rider's body leans over to the right simultaneously with the swerve, the momentum carries straight along on the original line; the grip alone has, therefore, to overcome this momentum. At a fast pace a very powerful muscular effort is required to stay in the saddle. If a horse rears, the body must go forward, otherwise the rider will lean towards the horse's quarters and may pull him over. Should the horse kick, the rider must lean the body back, or unless the grip is powerful, he will go over the horse's head.

In other words, the rider's body must conform with the horse's movements, but it must begin to do so a split second before the horse moves. The latter invariably gives warning of what he is going to do, and the sensitive rider has time to grip and adjust his balance. Those who fail in this particular come unstuck or save themselves by hanging on to the reins to the detriment of the horse's mouth. Recognition of these premonitory symptoms comes with riding experience. Beginners should, therefore, avoid what are called "quick horses".

A bus conductor, by long practice, acquires

instantaneous balance; he does not sit on his passengers nor grip the rail or strap no matter how quickly the vehicle alters pace or direction. Similarly, the budding horseman must cultivate this same balance. Some people think more quickly, some have keener sensitivity, but practice and determination to prevail will make these essentials fixed habits. Stirrups, by the way, greatly help balance, but too much reliance should not be placed on them.

The Germans have a striking phrase *"Immer mit"* —"always with". Be always with the horse. Balancing movements must be by the body from the waist upwards; the thighs, knees, legs and feet must stay put.

For those who desire a thorough grounding I advise a wooden horse, the introduction of which into the service was met with a deal of derision and opposition. However, it proved its worth a thousandfold. At that time I commanded a battery and my corporal rough rider disapproved of the innovation. When twelve recruits, who had never ridden, were posted, I let him pick six to teach in the old way. I took the remainder and started with the wooden horse. After three months, the colonel judged eleven of these recruits in the riding school. They were numbered and mixed up —one of my half-dozen was in hospital. They were put through an ordinary ride, with and without reins and stirrups, two plain fences and an in and out. My five took the first five places.

The corporal become an enthusiast for the wooden horse.

The great advantage of this inanimate steed is that the beginner can concentrate on all the preliminary essentials, position of the body, hands, arms, legs and feet, mounting and dismounting and exercising grip, without wondering, "What is going to happen next; what is the brute going to do?" Failing the wooden horse, though I believe some are still available, a really quiet, steady animal must be provided.

It may be considered a counsel of perfection, but to get the best results a covered school is essential. Six lessons in a covered school are worth more than a dozen in the open. In a school, the pupil realizes that the horse cannot get away. There are no onlookers to criticize, perhaps aloud. There should be two large mirrors on the wall, one at the side, the other at one end of the track. The latter must be hung high, so that the approaching horses do not see themselves. They must not be jumped towards it, otherwise they will shie off, thinking a collision is imminent. Riders should take full advantage of these mirrors to see how they look and so correct any apparent faults. Equally, when riding out, watch your reflections in the shop windows.

Failing a school, a manège is the next best thing, fenced in with a two-foot bank round it, built from a ditch on the outside, which facilitates drainage. The track should be of sand, tan or peat. A second railing outside the boundary fence makes a capital jumping lane. If no school or manège is available then a secluded field must suffice.

It is unfortunate that so many do not favour the school; believe me, it is most beneficial to both riders and horses, and not for beginners either. The instructor should always be mounted.

Mounting and Dismounting. Begin with these two all-important items. You can spot the "experts" by the way they approach and mount. To mount, go up to the horse quietly with a friendly word, a pat on the neck, if possible a tit-bit in the hand. Judge the sensitivity of the mouth by actuating the bit; see that the curb chain, in the case of a double bridle, is correctly twisted and fitted; that the bit or bits are not too high nor too low in the mouth, and that the throat lash is neither too tight nor too loose. This must be a ritual. Presumably the horse has been taught to stand still or is being held, but he is not likely to stand if a sharp toe is dug into his flank. Stand on the near side facing the tail, about level with the withers, lay the left hand, palm up, on the neck just clear of the withers, place the reins in that hand crossed as will be demonstrated, put whip or stick in the left hand and close it. With the right hand, take a lock of the mane, or mounting lock, and twist it twice anti-clockwise round the left thumb. There should now be the slightest but equal feel of both reins. If there is neither mane nor mounting lock, the left wrist can be crooked over the neck, or a grip taken of the pommel of the saddle. *On no account must the rein be used to help the rider up.*

The next step is to insert the left foot in the stirrup, giving it a twist, so that the inside of the foot, not the toe, is against the horse's flank and the right hand gets hold of the off side of the cantle. Leaning slightly forward and giving a hop with the right foot, carry the right leg over the horse's quarters, keeping it only slightly bent, move the right hand to the off side of the pommel to take some of the weight. Don't straighten the left leg and oil into the saddle, and don't land with a squelch as so many do. Do not despise a mounting block. In the case of a tall horse, a short leg and perhaps badly-cut breeches, it is a good idea to let the near side leather down a hole or two. Learn how to take a "leg up". If young and active, you can vault on, or at least, like a stable lad, jump the body on to the withers, then cock the right leg over. Later on, practise mounting from the off side and train the horse to take it.

It is most useful to change horses without dismounting. Have the second horse brought up on the off side, take both feet out of the stirrups, place right hand on the pommel of the second horse and your left foot under you, with your left hand on your pommel give a lift with both hands and left foot, raise the right leg and carry it over the second horse, landing gently on the saddle of the second horse. Whatever method of mounting is adopted, there must be no jerks or bumps, the reins must be taken up with a gentle feel. A pause for a moment or two, after the length of the leathers is adjusted, then move off. If several riders are going out, no one must move until all are mounted and ready.

To dismount—naturally the converse of mounting—have reins with whip or stick in the left hand placed on pommel, right hand alongside the left on off side. Slip the right foot quietly out of the iron and swing the right leg fairly straight over the horse's quarters. Lower the right foot to the ground and take the left foot out of the stirrup, taking care that the toe does not dig into the horse. In the case of a tall horse, it will probably be necessary to slip the left foot out of the iron, as the right foot comes over, taking the weight on the hands.

There are several other ways of dismounting, voluntarily and otherwise! By taking both feet out of the irons take the weight on the hands and vault off, or, with both feet out, throw the right leg over in front of the saddle, sit sideways and slide down, taking care not to catch the heel in the iron. Never wave the right hand in the air, especially if you have neglected to pass the whip or stick into the left hand: the horse may think that you are threatening him and act accordingly. Also practise dismounting on the off side.

Mounting and dismounting are most important; so many riders are haphazard and clumsy about this. Never leave your mount without a kindly word, a pat on the neck and, if possible, a titbit. A crust in the pocket is the mark of a good horseman.

How to Sit in the Saddle. This phrase sums up the matter: sit *in* the saddle, not *on* the saddle. The good horseman gets down into the saddle and appears to be part and parcel of the horse. The rider must sit fairly and squarely to his front, the body leaning forward, just the least trifle inside the perpendicular. Shoulders neither humped nor rounded, head neither poked forward nor thrown back, eyes looking between the horse's ears. If a hat is worn, as it always should be, let it have a slight forward tilt.

The arms should hang loosely, the elbows nicely into the flanks above the hips, never stuck out. The forearm should be as nearly as possible horizontal, inclined a trifle inwards, knuckles nearly vertical, wrists rounded and supple, with fingers closed. From the hips upwards, the body must give to the horse's movements, being at all times ready to balance.

The Legs. There is an old saying, "Keep a leg each side, and you can't come off." True—but to do so, position, balance, and grip must be right.

The Thigh. Should be at such an angle to the lower leg as will enable the rider to get right down comfortably into the saddle, get a good grip above the knee, and allow the knee to be in constant contact with the saddle-flap.

The Knee is all important; its inside surface must be fixed to the saddle. Never let it lose touch; that is a cardinal fault. A tight grip is not necessary all the time, but the rider must be ready to apply it the moment it becomes necessary; not with a sudden jerk, which is apt to upset a horse, but with a squeeze.

The Lower Leg. Should hang down nearly straight from the knee, just a trifle drawn back, the inside of the calf against the saddle flap. If the rider, without pushing his head forward, can just see his toe, past the point of the knee, the position is correct.

The Feet must not be stuck out at an angle from the horse, but be as nearly parallel to the flank as conformation will permit. With the point of the knee as near the saddle-flap as may be, the foot will not be far out. The toe must be kept up, the heel down. In that position the muscles are in pronation, the grip strong; in the reverse position they are in supination, the grip weak.

The Leathers. What length should they be? Some advocate the short seat, others the medium or long one. Of course, the short seat is universal for racing on the flat or over a country. Personally I plump for the medium every time. With the short seat the aids cannot be properly applied, you can't keep a horse straight, or school a young one, and at Polo it cramps your stroke. The long seat is good when long distances have to be covered and most prefer it for dressage. A compromise is best, neither too long nor too short, in fact a utility seat, which answers well for hunting, hacking, show jumping, polo, breaking and schooling.

(See Plate I. Two good examples of the UTILITY SEAT.)

A rider should learn to gauge the length by measuring leather plus iron with the arm before mounting. Naturally, the leathers must be level; they should be frequently changed from one side to the other, as constant mounting and dismounting on the near side causes the leathers to stretch.

A narrow horse generally needs a hole shorter, a broad one a hole longer. It is essential that a rider should learn as early as possible whether the leathers are the right length or not. At first the instructor, if there is one, will help him. Nothing is so unworkmanlike as a rider fussing over the length and calling on others to make alterations. The horseman just presses down, maybe rising off the saddle just once, then if any alteration is needed, sees to it himself.

To Shorten. Disengage the leg towards the rear only just sufficiently to let the hand get to the leather. Place the back of the hand towards the saddle, grip the free end of the leather in the palm,

I. TWO EXAMPLES OF GOOD UTILITY SEATS

thumb on the tongue of the buckle. Keep the foot in the iron, ease it up a trifle, a pull on the leather, a little pressure on the tongue of the buckle with the back of the first finger will disengage the tongue. As you pull on the leather move the hand up, keeping the thumb close up and the first finger against the tongue. As the tongue comes opposite the required hole, ease the hand and let it engage, press down on the iron.

To Lengthen. Take hold of the leather as above, disengage the tongue, then press a trifle on the stirrup, at the same time easing the leather, keeping the thumb on the next hole. When it comes opposite the tongue let it engage. That will be one hole down. You can let out as many more as may be required in the same way. A little further pressure on the stirrup drives the tongue well home.

In both operations make sure that the buckle is up against the bar, then tuck the end under the leather pointing the rear.

At first it will be necessary to look down and watch what you are doing, but intelligent practice will enable one to do it blind after a time. When in company, it is irritating for the others to have to wait while a rider is having his leathers adjusted.

Stirrups. The tread should be kept well roughened. The irons should be neither too broad nor too narrow for the foot. This is a vital matter. It is difficult for riding schools and livery stables to cater for all sizes. Some riders very wisely bring their own irons. Very small children should have shoe stirrups, older children safety stirrups, all saddles must have safety bars. In my opinion the foot should be home, though some prefer the stirrup on the broad of the foot. With the foot in the stirrup it is now essential to get that kink in the ankle which works right up to the knee through the lower part of the leg, lowers the inside edge of the sole and raises the outside edge. This sounds formidable, but *if the sole of the foot is turned slightly outwards*, you will feel the knee working right into the saddle-flap.

The Downward Thrust. This may be called the finishing touch by which the rider gets right down into the saddle. Press well down evenly on both irons, kink the ankles, press the knee point tight into the saddle. This should be constantly practised at the halt and on the move.

Some horses blow themselves out when being girthed up. In any case it is as well to test your girths after you have been out for a bit and tighten if necessary. Keep the foot in the stirrup, cock the leg just sufficiently forward to clear the flap, raise it, take hold of one girth strap in the full of the hand back towards the horse, forefinger against the tongue of the buckle. Take a pull and guide the tongue into the required hole. Then the other strap. Practise this a lot on both sides—you must be able to do it without looking down.

CHAPTER III

THE INDEPENDENT SEAT

HAVING defined the essentials of a good seat we may now move on.

All horses and ponies should be provided with a neck strap, fitted loosely round the neck, just in front of the withers. A stirrup leather does quite well, but should there be a leather shortage a thin rope such as a clothes-line will suffice. This fitting is intended as a safety-line, for use when a rider is a bit unsteady or lacking in confidence, but it must not be allowed to become a habit. It is there only as a last resort.

Beginners should not be hurried. The start should be with stirrups, the correct position being strictly insisted upon. The reins should be dropped as soon as possible, arms folded, left hand gripping right biceps, right hand back down holding left elbow. It is as well to keep the full of the reins in the right hand to prevent them from flopping about, also so that they can be quickly taken up if necessary.

"Grip—Ease—Grip—Ease", should be practised, until the muscles begin to tire. Then "Relax"— "Rest". After a short rest the correct position must be resumed. More "Grip"—"Ease", a few turns, and so on.

As soon as the seat appears to be settled, the stirrups should be quitted and crossed in front of the saddle, the correct position being carefully adhered to.

The Trot. When the novice appears to be comfortable in the saddle, and doing well at the walk, a gentle trot should be tried, with stirrups and reins to start with, which should be dispensed with as soon as possible. In the school or manège, with a steady leader, this is quite safe, otherwise the instructor must lead the pupil. The moment the toe goes down and the position is lost, the order to walk must be given and the seat regained. At the outset only short spells without stirrups should be indulged in, lengthened gradually as grip strengthens and confidence grows. A good bit of bumping round at the trot will go a long way towards the acquisition of grip and balance.

Then comes rising at the trot—with stirrups, of course. By degrees rhythm will come; no strenuous effort is required. The horse's hind action must raise the rider, who only assists with a bit of grip and pressure on the irons. The knee and the lower leg must stay put, head and feet must not waggle. If difficulty is experienced without the reins, a little assistance from the neck strap may be permitted, this to be discontinued as early as possible, otherwise the rider will acquire the habit of rising with the aid of the reins. When coming down, the seat must meet the saddle without a bump.

Having got the hang of the rise, the learner should learn to change. Say the rise is on the near hind, bump once, then rise on the off hind. This does not sound easy, but watch the instructor do it and it is quite simple. Such changes ease the horse on a long hack. If there is no instructor it is suggested that the learner should study what is written here and apply the lesson himself.

Canter. Once the seat is fairly well established, the next step is to canter, which is really the easiest pace of all. At first the tendency is to bump up and down, but this can soon be overcome by sitting down into the saddle, leaning neither back nor forward, just inside the perpendicular, with a nice easy grip, a bit of downward thrust, knee, lower leg and foot kept well in place and ankle kinked.

Before the canter is attempted the novice should have plenty of practice at standing up in the stirrups, gripping the while, firstly at the halt, then at the trot. A hand on the neck strap may be permitted at first to help matters.

As soon as the canter with stirrups is satisfactory, cantering without them should be tried and persevered with.

Gallop. Of course, sooner or later, everybody will want to gallop. The position is exactly the same as for the canter, except that the rider's seat should be raised just clear of the saddle and the grip increased. Body bent slightly forward, back neither hollow nor rounded. Reins should be shortened somewhat, hands kept low. The tension on the reins will, of course, depend on the horse, but should not be used to help raise the seat off the saddle and keep it there. There must, of course, be a certain pressure on the irons, but not to the extent that should a leather break, disaster would result.

Normally the gallop would start from the canter. Later on a rider should be able to jump into a gallop from a walk or even from the halt, but only when there is no danger of being left behind, resulting in the horse's mouth being jabbed.

So far I have recommended the use of the saddle, but once a certain stage of proficiency has been attained, a lot of work should be done on a numnah, which will help and improve balance a great deal. Bare-back is perhaps better, but some horses have rather sharp backbones, so numnah let it be. The secret of sitting successfully on the numnah is to ride as much as possible by balance, only gripping when necessary.

Falls at the initial stage do a lot of harm, some beginners being permanently discouraged. Stupid instructors and some grooms will tell them that they must take a large number of tosses before they can ride. That is nonsense as far as the novice is concerned. It is true that one must expect a certain number when hunting, schooling, breaking and so on, during which experience one is all the time learning; but falls should be avoided until the rider has gained confidence and has passed the elementary stage. It is not possible to lay down any cut-and-dried course, so much depends on a particular pupil's progress. But a good bit of bumping round at the trot with and without stirrups will help a great deal.

Riding small ponies bare-back is also excellent practice; because of their being small there is nothing to grip below the knee, therefore all the more balance is required; moreover, they are generally a bit quick in the turns.

I adopted a practice many years ago which produced very satisfactory results. Pupils worked in pairs, one mounted without reins and stirrups, the other driving the horse on the long reins, which should be fastened to the head collar and passed through the stirrups, behind the leg of the rider. Five minutes each will be found sufficient if the horse is kept at the trot. Of course, if there is only one pupil, the instructor or a friend must do the driving. A halt must be called if the rider looks like coming unstuck.

The foregoing practices will most undoubtedly produce the correct seat, with the needful grip and balance, but if carried out more or less to the letter this method is certainly the hard way: the hard way is the best way. But, as these days the tendency is to go the easy way, it may be necessary to modify my system considerably. Many pupils at riding schools seem to want only to learn enough to stick on more or less, assisted by the reins, and think that if they can do so they are well enough equipped to go hacking. If that is their ambition, then reins and stirrups may have to be given somewhat earlier than I recommend. With children, lessons should not be too tedious. A spot of fun, chasing each other to snatch a handkerchief, or gymkhana events, can be indulged in to finish up the lesson.

But those who intend to take up horsemanship as a profession or who really mean business should read, mark, learn and inwardly digest and practise what I am venturing to preach in this book. Much can be done alone or, better still, with a friend. Though, of course, best of all is in the school or manège, under a good instructor.

The reins must *never* be used as a means of support. If this is permitted at the outset, it will become a fixed habit, terribly hard to eradicate. Such riders may easily join the undesirable company of "straphangers". What a lot of them are in evidence and "Oh", the poor horse. No wonder his lot and his mouth are hard.

The Seat must be Independent of the Reins.
This simply means that the rider can stay in the saddle entirely by grip and balance; *then and only then can he or she hope to have Good Hands.* Children should be entered as early as possible to the bare back and encouraged to drop their reins. See Plate II.

As proficiency increases there is no better practice

than a bit of drill in a fair-sized field or on the sands, with plenty of right and left turns. Now, if a rider wishes to satisfy himself or herself that the seat is truly independent, let him or her canter down the school or manège without reins or stirrups, blind-folded or with eyes shut. On arrival at the end, the horse will naturally turn, and then, if the rider is *"immer mit"*, without applying leg aids, all is well. If this test is considered a bit too severe, a rider may try it first with his eyes open and perhaps a loose rein. But the shut eyes are the acid test. The diffi-culty these days is the question of time and money. Owing to the fantastic cost of everything, riding schools and livery stables have had to raise their charges, but it is possible that a reduction may be arranged, provided that a certain number engage to take a given number of rides or lessons in the form of classes, which could be carried out, say, in the evenings or early morning.

I strongly recommend an intensive course, either as a paying or working student, even during a holiday. *But the school must be carefully selected.* Those who intend to make it a career must be prepared to put in, some say a year, I recommend two, and after that it is a life study.

Exercises. To improve the seat and get the gripping muscles strong and keep them so, it is essential to carry out the necessary exercises.

Mounted. (1) At the halt, without reins and

stirrups. Arms folded, lean right back until head touches croup—knee and foot must stay put—then back into the upright position.

(2) Arms above the head, bend over on near side till tips of fingers of both hands touch left toe, then back again to upright position.

(3) Ditto, ditto, but down to off side and right foot.

(4) Swing the arms round first to the front then to the back, keeping the body absolutely steady.

(5) Keeping the knee in position, swing the foot backward and forward, parallel to the horse's side. Keep the body absolutely steady. This exercise helps to apply the aids without displacing the knee.

These exercises can be carried out on the wooden horse, thus saving the hire of the live animal.

Dismounted. (1) Lie on the back, on bed or floor, hands behind the head, elbows square. Raise the right leg say 18 inches, swing it slowly to the right as far as it will go, then back across and over the left leg as far as possible. The leg must be kept straight with toe pointed. The left leg must not move, nor must there be any rolling movement of the body.

(2) Repeat the process with the left leg. A dozen such movements, with each leg, should be the minimum.

(3) Raise both legs slowly, quite straight, toes pointed and pressed close together. When the legs are about 60°, separate the feet, and move them

with a downward circular motion, bringing them together when about 12 inches from floor or mattress, then raise legs as before and repeat circular motion.

(4) Raise both legs straight and pressed together until the feet are 12 inches up, then separate feet and move them upwards in a circular motion, until they meet when the legs are about 60°. Then lower legs till feet are 12 inches up and repeat. In (3) and (4) the motions must be very slow; 12 of each, should be aimed at.

(5) Sit on a high chair, end of sofa or some similar seat, so that the knees are bent at about the same angle as when in the saddle, heels on the ground, toes slightly raised and ankles kinked. Place the clenched fists in prolongation and grip them with the knees. Then Squeeze—Ease—Squeeze— Ease, until the muscles begin to tire.

(6) Get a friend to stand facing you, say two feet apart, both right hands holding the backs of two chairs. Advance both left feet and let them engage, legs straight and stiff. Then on the word "go", each try to push the other's left foot out to the left. Then move the chairs round and compete with the right legs. Don't overstrain.

In addition, there is an excellent exerciser with strong elastic which is first-class for the riding muscles and also for the arms, as well as for the rest of the body.

Or a simple contraption can be rigged with weights and pulleys.

41

It will be found that if the above exercises are persevered with, the riding muscles will become really strong; stiffness after riding will disappear and, above all, the danger of rider's strain will be reduced to a minimum.

The Saddle. So much for the seat; but the saddle plays an important rôle. In the first place, *it must fit the horse*, but it must also fit and suit the rider. It must be long enough in the seat and sufficiently cut forward to provide ample knee room. It is a great mistake to ride in a very light saddle in order to keep down the weight. A narrow waist lets the rider down more into the saddle. Small children should always be put on narrow ponies. Their saddles should be narrow in the waist. Numnah and sheepskin saddles are also very suitable. A chat with your saddler is the best way to learn about saddles and to get one to suit you. All the saddlers that I have known, and they are many, were right good fellows, loved a chat, and were always only too pleased to assist and instruct.

If, however, as may happen in the case of riding schools or livery stables, the saddle supplied is not all that might be desired, have it changed before starting out. If this is not possible, make the best of it, do not bore companions all the way out and back with its shortcomings.

I fear that some may consider that I have unduly laboured the question of grip, balance and seat. But when we consider the enormous number of bad seats there are, legs, feet, hands, bodies all over the place, children trailing along behind a teacher and sitting all anyhow, one finds it unnecessary to apologize for insisting on these matters.

Plate I gives good samples of the utility seat.

CHAPTER IV

THE REINS

Reins Position. Reins in both hands. The first essential is correct position. We have already got the arm hanging easily from the shoulder, neither tight to the sides, nor yet stuck out, forearm practically horizontal, hands kept as low as possible. The hands should be so far apart, as to keep the reins clear of the neck. If the hands are kept well apart the pull is slightly outwards and thus the rings or sides of the bit are clear of the corners of the mouth.

Now comes the important part of the position (see Plate II). With a double bridle the little finger separates them. Some have the curb rein on the outside, some the snaffle. It depends which you wish to actuate first when the little finger is turned towards the body. The reins come up through the full of the hand, pinched principally by the third and little finger, and finally by the thumb. The stick or whip is held in the full of the hand, generally the right. The wrists are slightly rounded. Give and take is brought about by bringing the knuckles vertical for give, bringing the little finger nearer the body and turning the hand over for take. If and when more take is required, then the wrists are brought into play assisted by the arms. The action

44

of the wrists is similar to that of the top joint of a
fishing rod.

It is a good dodge to fix a bridle or at least a
double rein with a bit of elastic to two hooks and to
sit down and practise this position. Or, better still,
get someone to sit opposite you, holding the bit or
rein, ready to criticize, advise and assist.

A very usual fault is what is known as hands
back up. In this position there is invariably a dead
pull, the supple give and take of the wrist is absent,
resulting in a heavy hand. Naturally there must be
an even tension on both reins, which means an
equal feeling on both sides of the mouth.

With a light-mouthed horse, restraint can be
achieved by little finger towards the body, so tightening the reins and actuating the bit. But with harder
mouths, no matter what force has to be applied,
the wrist must be kept bent, so obviating that hard,
harsh straight pull, which spells bad hands.

In the initial stages the novice will be quite busy
getting a seat and staying on. It is a mistake to
overtax; therefore as much rein drill as possible
should be done on the wooden horse or dismounted
until the proper positions and actions become a fixed
habit. It is a good plan to have the curb rein just a
trifle narrower than the snaffle. This obviates confusion. The width of the reins should be propor-
tional to the size of the hands—this is important,
especially for ladies and children. Small hands
cannot handle wide reins either comfortably or
efficiently.

It is a good plan to let children ride on a snaffle, with a short curb rein lying on the pony's neck just in front of the withers; then, if the pony is starting to go a bit too strong, the bit rein can be taken up and more control obtained.

In One Hand. Although, with both hands on the reins, the flexible wrist and correct hand finger movement give a lighter and more delicate touch, it is sometimes restful to change to one hand, as has to be done for opening a gate and for other reasons. It is essential that the change should be effected neatly, easily and precisely. The reins all festooned in and around one hand are a distressing sight.

There are several methods of holding the reins in one hand, but one is quite sufficient. I have therefore selected that which I have found the easiest, simplest and most efficient. This is set out in Plate II.

With the single rein, the majority of riders, when riding with reins in both hands, bring it round outside the little finger, up through the full of the hand, securing it with all four fingers and thumb. Some, however, bring it through between the little and third finger, then up through the hand, the idea being that if so held it is less liable to slip.

To Change from One Hand to Both Hands. Say from left hand. Place the right hand a few inches in front of the left, insert the little finger between the offside reins, pinch the near side reins

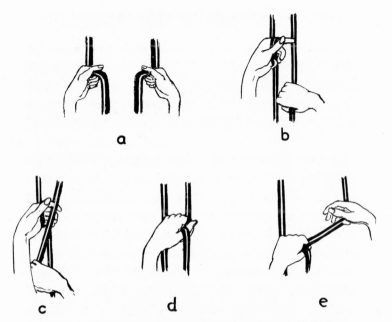

II. TO CHANGE REINS INTO THE LEFT HAND

a—Reins in both hands. Double bridle. Snaffle rein on the outside.

b—Bring back the right hand well behind the left, turning it over back up. This brings the snaffle rein uppermost. Gripping the left rein between thumb and base of first finger, extend first finger. Move right hand to the left, bringing the first finger of the left hand between the two right reins.

c—Then open the fingers of the left hand, lower the right hand so bringing the reins into the full of the left hand, which closes immediately. The left hand should not move. The right hand ensures that the feel on both sides of the mouth is equal.

d—Reins in left hand, snaffle reins outside.

e—From reins in left hand to take reins into both hands. Advance the right hand well in front of the left, back up and fingers open, place little finger between right reins.

Take both right reins in the full of the right hand, grip the left reins between thumb and base of first finger. Slide the right hand back level with the left which releases the right rein.

tight between the thumb and root of first finger of the left hand. Open left hand, releasing off-side rein, slide right back, taking up off-side reins into the full of the hand, close both hands and the change is completed.

In all these operations, contact and "feel" must never be lost.

To change from the right hand to both hands, again for "left" read "right".

With a single rein it is even simpler. You do not have to use the little finger, the one rein is simply taken outside the little finger and into the full of the hand.

To Shorten the Reins. With the reins in both hands, starting with the left. Take hold of the reins with first finger and thumb of right hand, pull them through, until desired shortening is acquired. Then do the same to the off-side reins, with first finger and thumb of left hand. The hand in which the reins are being shortened must stay put.

To Lengthen. Simply relax the grip, slide the hand back and let the rein slip till the required length is reached. Do one hand at a time. Contact and feel must be maintained.

To Shorten the Reins in One Hand. Say the left. The right hand can be used to pull first the near-side rein through the hand, then drop below the left hand and pull the off-side rein, until the required amount of rein is obtained. Or, the reins can be taken up in both hands, the near-side rein shortened with the right hand, while gripping the off-side tightly with three fingers; take hold of the near-side reins just above the left hand with thumb and first finger, left hand then releases grip and right hand pulls until required length is attained. Right hand then passes its reins back to the left hand, shortening from behind, until level with near-side rein. With reins in right hand simply reverse process.

To lengthen with reins in one hand, say the left. Grip the near-side reins tightly with left thumb, ease up the fingers, take the off-side rein in the full of the right hand in front of the left hand and pull them a little till the reins are sufficiently lengthened, then pinch them between left thumb and forefinger. Now, place right hand again in front of the left, take hold of the near-side reins in the full of the hand, relax the three fingers of the left hand, pull the near-side reins, until level with off-side reins, then close left hand.

Or, change into both hands, lengthen as required and change back to one hand. This is the method I prefer, as it maintains contact and gets the required length better.

By gripping the reins with second finger and fourth fingers, you can free the thumb and first finger and use them for manipulating the reins in the other hand. In all the foregoing rein movements, with a double rein, quite a bit of grip can be exercised between the third and little finger.

Sticks and Whips. A stick or whip may be carried when hacking but it must not be a hunting whip without a thong. If hacking with dogs which need more than voice control, a hunting whip with a thong may be carried. In summer I prefer a fly-whisk. It is essential to carry a stick or whip correctly.

A stick should be held in the full of the hand, about the centre, pointing across the body; a cutting whip near the base, point downwards; a hunting whip in the full of the hand with thong against it, rest of thong hanging down. Dismounted, the thong should be brought up in a loop. It can also be carried when mounted, this way, but it is rather a handful. Do not carry it like a fishing rod.

When hunting, a thong is essential. To show the thong to, far less use it on, a hound, is one of the unforgivable sins, unless, once in a lifetime perhaps, a rider may be in that fortunate position as to be asked to turn hounds. All who hunt should, therefore, be able to crack a whip. All hunters should be trained to "stand a whip" as it is called. The handle is, of course, necessary for opening gates and this should be practised.

At the risk of being irrelevant I must protest against a hunting whip being called a crop. I suppose it is on par with "pink". I have never known a Master or hunt servant use either of these terms. The rules laid down for hunt dress, *vide* Bailey, most certainly do not specify "pink".

It is absolutely essential to bring the handling of

the reins to perfection. To start with it must be carried out dismounted as recommended earlier in this chapter. At first it will be necessary to look down and watch the proceedings, but by degrees it can be carried out blind. Take it step by step, get one movement absolutely right before moving on to the next. When out hacking, keep on changing reins, stick and whip, until it is so easy as to be second nature. It is pitiful to see some riders endeavouring to open a gate. They suddenly find that they have got the reins in both hands; they fumble nervously, one rein escapes, the others hang in festoons. The workman changes into the required hand before he reaches the gate, gets the whip to work, swings the gate open, perhaps gives it a bit of a kick with his foot, holds it until the next rider comes up; and then off. When it is necessary to change stick, hunting whip or cutting whip from one hand to the other: assume reins are in left hand and stick or whip in the right—to change it to the left hand, first change the reins to the right hand, then pinch in all the reins tightly with the thumb, open the fingers just sufficiently to allow the left hand to withdraw the whip or stick. The other way on, when changing left hand to right. There is no point in changing with both hands on the reins, a change is only necessary when stick or whip is needed for use.

"Picking up" a cutting whip cannot be learnt from a book or diagram. If needed, the only way is to get a jockey or a G.R. or other expert to show you, then practise. But the less a whip or stick is used on a horse the better.

Some riders, particularly when show jumping, like to cross the reins and rest them on the horse's neck, just in front of the withers, with a hand each side of the neck. This undoubtedly brings a certain amount of the weight further forward. To cross the reins, reins being in both hands: take hold of the near-side reins in the full of the right hand, pinching the off-side reins with the thumb and base of fore-finger; slide along until the hands are 12 inches apart, then grip. Next, take the ends of the off-side reins in the full of the left hand, pinching the near-side reins between the thumb and base of fore-finger; slide along until this rein is tight. During this operation care must be taken that contact with both sides of the bit is maintained.

There is another tip which can be usefully employed if the reins become too wet, sodden and slippery to grip. With both hands on the reins, gripping the near-side reins as tightly as possible with all the fingers of the left hand, with the thumb and fore-finger of the right hand wind the rein or reins once round the left thumb. Then, while pinching the rein or reins by the thumb against the base of the first finger, open the other fingers and pass the end of the reins down the full of the hand and close the fingers. In the same way repeat the process with the thumb of the right hand. When held like this the reins certainly will not slip, nor can they be quickly released. The one objection is that if a horse pecks rather heavily you probably will be pulled right over his head, as happened to me on one memorable occasion.

With an instructor or assistant holding the bits or end of reins, you get the necessary criticism and instruction; but, if on your own, it is a good plan to fix up a mirror so that you can see and criticize yourself. With the book and figures before you proficiency can soon be attained, then keep on practising whenever you ride out. Until you can do all the changes without looking down, you are still in the novice stage.

Contact. There is a good deal of talk these days about this essential. When all is said and done it simply means that a rider, through the reins, has a continual and light feel on the horse's mouth. The importance of this is that, when the reins are actuated the pressure is gradual, i.e., there is no jab in the mouth as would happen if the reins were loose. A more subtle and essential reason for insistence on contact is that the horse, well-mannered and mouthed, will go nicely up to his bridle, just feeling it, neither pulling nor leaning on it (i.e., in front of his bridle). If he is a slug or too harshly bitted he will be "behind his bridle".

It is obvious that, with a nice contact, a horse going up to his bridle will respond to a slight easing of the reins and accelerate, or to a slight feel of the bit decrease speed. His turns will be smooth; in fact, it means a perfect and delightful control.

THE REINS

The French have a beautiful expression, *chercher la bride*, meaning look for or hunt the bridle. This exactly describes the perfect state of affairs, a horse always just feeling for his bit.

Many people say up to, in front of, or behind his bit, which is just as correct as bridle. When just hacking about, it is not necessary to maintain contact all the time. When walking along give yourself and the horse a rest, slope along now and then with a loose rein, but beware of being taken by surprise.

Contact is apt to be overdone. Riders are frequently to be seen pushing their hands forward, then drawing them back, with the mistaken idea that they are achieving perfect contact and/or assisting to mouth the horse.

If the movement of the horse's head is carefully noted at the walk, it will be seen that it moves naturally forward and back a very short distance; therefore, to maintain a nice contact, the hands should only give and take exactly that same amount. Wrist movement is sufficient and should hardly be noticeable. In faster paces, contact must synchronize with the horse's head and leg movement, but again the hands do not need to move to any extent.

Now, it is all very well to talk about contact with a perfectly-mannered horse. There aren't so many about, particularly in riding schools and livery stables. If a horse is in front of his bridle, look for the reason: he may be pulling or leaning because you are laying hold of him, in which case give him a

53

lighter hand and *don't strap hang*. He may be a light mouth puller because the bit is too sharp and hurts him. Give him a lighter bit and/or a lighter hand. He may have a hard, dead mouth, requiring a sharper or more severe bit, or he may have acquired a habit of leaning on the bit, caused by a succession of straphangers. Refuse to carry his face for him, raise the hands, give the reins a sharp tweak or two and he will soon mend his manners.

If a horse is "behind his bridle" because he is shy of it have an easier one substituted. Let him go with a loose rein for a while, then gradually gain contact, coaxing him up to his bit, and keeping him there with the legs. If he is a slug, then a pair of spurs is indicated.

Of course, with livery stables it is difficult to keep the horses' mouths anything like up to a decent standard. The poor old hireling is fated to be pulled about. With riding schools it should be much easier. If the chief instructor knows his or her job, the assistants and more advanced pupils should be employed largely in mouthing and remouthing, flexing and keeping the horses up to the mark generally. Where this is not done the implication is that they do not know how.

It comes to this: our endeavour must be to get the horse to understand that if he "gives" to the pressure of the bit and reduces speed he is rewarded by the pressure being lessened or ceasing.

CHAPTER V

BITS AND BITTING

THE hands control the horse's movements to a great extent by acting on the mouth, through the bit and reins. All the same it is essential closely to examine just how the bit functions.

There are bits of every shape, but it is my considered opinion that only a small number are needed to cope with ninety-nine mouths out of a hundred. In the long run hands matter more than bits.

Riders should study for themselves the action of each kind of bit. Stand alongside the horse, actuate the reins with one hand, raise the lips with the other so as to get a good view of what goes on in the horse's mouth. Ease and pull, rein him back, let the curb chain out a link or two, take it up a link or two. Watch the effect of both these adjustments on the bars and on the tongue. Work at the ordinary double bridle, at the pelham, half-moon and straight bar and bar with a port. Work the snaffle both jointed and straight. You will then have gained a thorough insight into the mouths and that knowledge will greatly help the acquisition and improvement of hands.

It is extraordinary how many riders, some who had ridden quite a lot, have not the faintest idea as to what happens in a horse's mouth when the bit is brought into play, nor had they ever attempted to find out.

A chat with a saddler, or an inspection of bits with an instructor in a riding school will provide sufficient insight into the art and aims of the Loriner.

The bars of the mouth are the two portions of the gums without teeth, except for the tush of a horse between the molar or back teeth and the incisors or front teeth.

It is true that there is a key to every horse's mouth, but much depends on the hands that turn the key. Let us look at some of these keys.

The Snaffle. We have (1) the jointed snaffle. This has rather a nut-cracker action. When the reins are in play it will be seen that this bit gives quite a lot of tongue room, while acting on the corners of the mouth and on the bars and to some extent on the tongue. With a callous mouth, a twisted snaffle or even a chain snaffle is often used. Naturally these are much more severe.

(2) Straight bar or half-moon snaffle. This is a good bit for a young and light-mouthed horse. It is kinder than the jointed snaffle. The hands should be kept low, or a rather short standing martingale should be used to insure that the pressure comes on the bars and tongue. I prefer the half-moon, it

gives more tongue room. An indiarubber snaffle is excellent to encourage a horse that is behind his bit to go up to it and take hold, or in the case of a light-mouthed puller. As it bends it gives quite a bit of tongue room, but a horse must not acquire the habit of leaning on it. Also it is invaluable when a mutton-fisted rider has to be mounted. A vulcanite mouthpiece is also useful, particularly if shaped to give a bit of tongue room. But it is not as easy as rubber.

(3) Gag snaffle is of use when a horse bores or insists on carrying his head low. It can be used either in conjunction with a curb bit or snaffle. Its action is similar to that of a bearing rein, but it is much more humane, being only actuated as and when the horse tries to get his head down. All snaffles should have big rings which help to turn the horse by pressing on the sides of the mouth and which also prevent the snaffle being pulled through the mouth. The thicker the mouthpiece the easier the bit.

The Pelham. Taken all round is a most useful bit and was adopted by the Army in preference to the old double bridle. It has a fairly thick movable mouthpiece with a low port, two emplacements for the bit rein, middle and bottom bar, one side of mouthpiece smooth and the other rough; it can be made mild or severe as one puts the bit rein on the middle or bottom bar, or uses the rough side if the horse's mouth is not as sensitive as it should be. A horse plays with a movable mouthpiece. I have found that most horses are happier with only one mouthpiece. You can do almost as much with the rein on the cheek as with the snaffle of the double bridle. Of course, for mouthing or making, the double is unrivalled. With the old Army bit I found I could hold horses and ponies comfortably that were a handful on other bits.

The half-moon Pelham is also a very useful bit, and on the easy side most horses go kindly in it.

With Pelhams the upper rein, i.e. on the cheek, acts on the mouthpiece exactly in the same way as the straight bar or half-moon snaffle, while the lower rein on the bar, in conjunction with the curb chain, brings about a levering action by which the mouthpiece presses on the bars of the mouth and the tongue. The half-moon and mouthpiece with a port are easier since they give more tongue room.

Pelhams can be obtained with rubber or vulcanite mouthpieces; also jointed. The last—the jointed— is now seldom met with and is not recommended.

Double Bridle is simply a snaffle and a bit with a curb chain. The action of a bit is exactly the same as a Pelham's when actuated by the lower reins. The function of this bridle is that the snaffle controls the carriage of the head, while the bit produces the flexions and so dictates the pace. When the bit rein is brought into play, the cheek, in conjunction with the curb chain, acts as a lever, bringing the mouthpiece on to the bars of the mouth and tongue. The severity of this action depends on the length of the cheek and the tightness of the curb chain. There are a variety of mouthpieces, but the best and simplest is one, not too thin, with a port not too high and wide enough to give tongue room. A straight mouthpiece is much too severe and gives no tongue room. A half-moon mouthpiece is quite useful and easy, while a movable mouthpiece lets the horse play with it.

It is absolutely essential that a horse should be comfortable with his bit or bits; they must fit properly. If a snaffle is too wide it will sag in his mouth. The snaffle must be fitted so that it is just up to the corners of his mouth without wrinkling it. The bit mouthpiece must rest about the middle of the bars, as a rule, one inch above the tush of a horse and two inches above the corner tooth of a mare. The curb chain requires close attention. It must be twisted up properly as from the near side clockwise, end link on hook thumb-nail up, fitting link thumb-nail down. The fitting of the curb chain is of the utmost importance as on its adjustment depends the severity of the bit.

A horse is seldom allowed to get sufficiently acquainted with his bit; it is only too often more or less forcibly thrust into his mouth. It is not surprising that he often resents it. It is therefore quite a good plan to put him on the short rack or pillar reins and let him stand for an hour or two each day with his bridle on. If he has a marked dislike to it, try dipping it in wet bran well powdered with sugar, before bitting up. If bran and sugar are not available, a light smear of "Golden Syrup" is a good substitute. In the case of a light-mouthed puller, I have found that the following solved the problem: take a Pelham and a strip of linen about two inches wide. Secure one end with thread at the near side, wind the strip along to the off side and then back again to the near side. Again securely fix it with thread. Damp the linen thoroughly, then smear with sugar if available; if not, a touch of syrup will make it acceptable.

As you will see when examining the action of the bit in the horse's mouth, the curb chain rests in the chin groove, which almost appears to be there on purpose. The chain should be fairly closely-linked; if too open it is apt to chafe. It is a good plan to have it protected with numnah or leather. Obviously, the longer the lower cheek of the bit, the greater will be the leverage; therefore the more severe will be the bit. The upper cheek should be short; if it is long the curb chain will be raised too high and will come in contact with the bone above the groove, and will almost certainly cause a rub. The lip strap should always be worn—there are emplacements on the lower cheek for it.

A noseband is very generally worn. Except for attachment to a standing martingale, it is of no practical use except that it makes the bridle look more dressed. It should be about two fingers below the projecting cheekbone, and neither too tight nor too loose. For some reason, sheepskin-covered nosebands have of late been worn on racehorses. If it is desired to keep the horse's mouth shut or to prevent his getting his tongue over the bit, a net should be fitted. The dropped noseband is a thin strap supported by the head stall. It is placed between the bit and snaffle, just sufficiently tight to keep the mouth shut. It is very useful for horses that give the lower jaw when the bit is actuated instead of the whole head by just opening the mouth. It is also useful for a hard puller. There is the Kineton noseband for really bad pullers which can be used either with a snaffle or special bit. It is so adjusted that it presses on the nose and stops the horse breathing. It requires careful fitting and is a saddler's job.

We sometimes hear that a horse took the bit between his teeth and bolted. What really happens is that a horse either raises or lowers his head to the extent that the pressure of the bit on the tongue and bars is relieved and the bit is actually up against the cornea teeth; i.e., the molars. This trick is undoubtedly acquired when a horse is wrongly handled when being broken. I have seen horses on the long reins going along with their heads well below their knees.

CHAPTER VI

THE AIDS

MANY look upon the Aids as a mystery, a secret known only to an enlightened few. This is quite wrong. The Aids and their application are perfectly simple. It is only necessary to get a complete understanding of their why and wherefore to be able to put them into practice.

It stands to reason that if we are to learn and be able to apply the Aids, it is essential that the horses on which we learn should be properly trained, have good mouths and be already responsive to the Aids. Any riding school worthy of the name should have a sufficient number of such mounts. Can anything be more pathetic than to watch a novice applying the legs, in accordance with the book, on a horse that hasn't the very faintest idea what it is all about! Students or pupils or their parents or advisers should make a point of visiting the school where it is proposed to learn the Aids and satisfy themselves by watching a ride under instruction that the horses and ponies are mouthed and mannered and that instruction is on sound lines.

Without the Aids a rider cannot really control his mount. He cannot modify or increase his pace, turn with safety, open a gate, balance a horse, bring him right to a fence, prevent him shying, or keep him straight. Such a rider is a third-class passenger and probably a straphanger as well. Having learnt the Aids and their application, a rider should practise them every time he goes out. Once proficient he can in due course teach them to a horse.

In examinations the question "What are the Aids?" is frequently asked. The answer is:

The Aids are of two kinds—(1) Natural, (2) Artificial.

(1) Natural—Hands, legs, body, voice
(2) Artificial—Bit, reins, martingale, whip, spurs.

By the Natural Aids we tell the horse what we want him to do.

The Artificial Aids simply help the Natural Aids. *E.g.* The bit and reins are necessary for the hands; the martingale corrects the carriage of the head so that the bit will bear on the bars of the mouth; the whip and spurs reinforce the leg pressure if and when required. By means of the Aids a horse is told what is required of him. To move from the halt. To halt when required. To regulate the pace when required. To turn, move sideways and rein back.

The Hands through the reins and bit control the forehand; i.e., head, neck, shoulders and to a certain extent the forelegs, as will be explained later.

The Legs control the hind-quarters and to some extent the fore legs by pressure against the horse's flank.

The Body controls by movement, backwards, forward or laterally, so shifting the centre of gravity. This movement should be hardly perceptible.

The Voice. In breaking, the voice should be used quite a lot. A rider, while refraining from continuous conversation with his mount, can use these aids at times; e.g., "Go on", "Steady", "Don't be a fool", "Whoa". But not much more. It is the tone that matters.

Bit and Reins. With hands as above.

Martingales are of three varieties.

(1) The *Running Martingale* is not of much use in keeping the head in the right position but gives some assistance in steering. Some authorities advise that the rings should be on the bit rein. Personally, I prefer them on the snaffle—this way you can sometimes coax a horse to lower his head a little; but if the head carriage has to be altered the answer is

(2) The *Standing Martingale*, attached to the noseband, not to the bit, just keeps his head in the right position, if fitted properly. Nowadays, it is a good deal used in show jumping and it is valuable in schooling. When a horse rises at a fence he should tuck his head in, which makes for better balance

and helps to get his hocks well under him. If he puts his head high as he is rising, his loin muscles become stiff; consequently, his hocks are not brought under him, he jumps off his forehand with his hind legs out behind, which is all wrong. As a rule, show riders generally slip the standing martingale before going for the water, as it is thought that it prevents a horse from stretching himself. Slow motion films do not bear out this contention.

(3) The *Irish Martingale* is simply a couple of rings joined by a piece of leather six to eight inches in length, through which the snaffle reins pass. As in the case of the running variety, it only helps in the steering and prevents the reins from going over the horse's head if and when he chucks his head about.

Whip. I do not recommend a whip, either as an Aid or as a punishment. It must not be forgotten that a horse can see quite a bit backwards. If a whip is used just as a horse is about to take off, his attention is taken off the fence. One has often seen a horse or pony simply dive through a fence when a whip was so used. Horses usually refuse to the left. This is because during schooling the rider's whip was in his right hand, the reins probably bunched in his left, the off rein slack. If a whip be applied, it must be put on as the hind legs are about to advance. A stroke then will undoubtedly lengthen the stride, but if applied as the stride is extended it has the effect of causing the horse to "curl up" and so shorten his stride. It requires the nicest judgment and years of experience to use a whip effectively. How many jockeys can really ride a whip finish? How many rogues have been created by the abuse of the whip? Apprentices are not allowed to carry them. Children should be similarly restricted in the show ring. If used at all the whip must be applied just behind the girth.

A long whip may be used to help the leg aids. An occasional "one for himself" is permissible with a slug, or a horse inclined to nap. But a whip should not be used when a horse shies. In a lifelong experience I have only had to have it out with three horses. In each case I had bought them as stallions and had them cut. We had a very serious argument but eventually they gave me best and I did not have to repeat the dose.

It is not a bad thing to show a horse the whip, but never if a tendency to halt or turn round is due to nervousness because of something he has seen or smelt. A horse's sense of smell is very acute and meeting a strange smell or one which recalls unpleasant memories may bother or perplex him.

Spurs. A rather controversial matter. With the very short seat the question does not arise. The main argument against, appears to be that the spur may be applied inadvertently. Surely this is a confession of weakness; personally I am all for the spur provided, of course, that the rider is such that the spur never goes in accidentally. With a horse, well-schooled and of such high sensitivity that the contraction of the leg muscles and the pressure of the inside of the calf have the desired effect, the spur is superfluous. But such paragons are few and far between. I always kept three varieties of spurs going. One pair dumb, one pair with blunt rowels, and a third pair with rather sharper rowels. I saw a good many old-time *Haute Ecole* masters on the Continent. They all wore box spurs and could play on a horse's flank as a skilled pianist plays on the keys. Spurs, if used, should be applied just behind the girth.

With good hands on both reins, a firm seat, strong legs and a knowledge of the Aids, a pair of spurs if required, and you are master of the situation.

So much for the Aids, now for their

Application. We are not discussing the art of breaking and/or training, but simply the application of the Aids when dealing with a horse that has been properly schooled.

It has been laid down that the hands (reins) govern the forehand and the legs the hind end. But to obtain the desired result, hands and legs must be operated in complete synchronization; if anything, the legs a fraction of a second before the hands.

It must always be remembered that a horse is a creature of habit: once he has been taught to obey the Aids he will do so without question.

Before considering how the legs govern the hind quarters, it is as well to examine carefully the movement of the horse's hind legs in action, or by photo-

graphs, preferably on a strip of film in slow motion.
At the walk and trot the hind legs move forward one
at a time; at the canter they follow each other in
more rapid succession; at the gallop still more
rapidly till they almost strike off simultaneously.

No matter at what pace, by means of that hind
foot the muscles of the hind leg and quarters produce the motive power which lifts the body and
sends it forward. This is termed PROPULSION. The
further forward the foot comes and the greater the
power used the longer will be the stride and faster
the pace. Obviously the horse's forelegs must conform with the hind legs or he would topple
over.

If the rider's legs are applied to the horse's sides,
just behind the girths at the exact moment when this
muscular effort is *about* to be made—a split second
later the reins must, of course, be eased—a longer
stride and a faster pace will result. This is a matter
of very nice timing. It is self-evident that if the
legs be applied after the hind foot has left the ground
the effort will have been made and the application
can have no effect on the muscular effort. It must,
therefore, be put on at exactly the right moment,
taken off and put on again. A rider soon senses the
hind movements at all paces; it is only a matter of
study, thought and practice. The force of application must be strictly in accordance with the sensitivity of the horse. A keen horse, with free forward
movement, needs gentle treatment; just a contraction of the muscles will suffice to increase speed,

whereas a slug requires more forceful methods, with even an application of the spur to remind him that the leg aid demands extra exertion on his part. This application of the leg is known as IMPULSION. In other words, sending him into his bit.

While IMPULSION is enormously important, there is a danger of its being over-emphasized and consequently overdone.

Too often a rider is to be seen going along with legs and heels bump-bumping on the horse's flanks, quite irrespective of what the hind legs are doing, under the mistaken impression that he is providing IMPULSION and producing PROPULSION.

At the gallop, to increase the effort as in riding a finish, the legs must be applied rather more vigorously but again timed to a nicety. Just as the legs increase the pace, so at the halt, by pressure, they can make a horse stand to attention by putting him up to his bit. Clearly, in the above examples, the hands must co-ordinate. This will be dealt with later.

The other use of the leg is by the pressure of one leg against the flank, as a rule just behind the girth, but it can be applied further back if the hind legs are not answering satisfactorily. This aid so applied causes the horse to move latterly, e.g. the application of the left leg causes the horse to move the near hind over to the right in front of the off hind. Though the near foreleg also has to move over to the right, by the action of the reins, as will be shown later, the application of the leg also has a certain influence.

The legs also control the hind quarters when turning and reining back. The leg must be applied without movement of the body or bobbing of the head, and the knees must be tight to the saddle.

The Body Aids play a more important part than is generally realized. By shifting the weight of the body from one side to the other, the side so relieved is lightened. Thus a horse finds it easier to lift and move the required leg. e.g. Right pass, shift the weight of the body to the off side. This reduces the weight on the near shoulder, near fore and hind legs, so, when the rein and leg aids are applied, it is easier for the horse to raise his near side feet than if the rider's weight had been evenly distributed on the saddle.

It is quite unnecessary to sway the body about, as is so often done when an attempt is made to change a leg at the canter. The desired effect can be better attained by just easing one hambone ever so little off the saddle, which automatically shifts the weight on to the other, at the same time reducing the pressure on the stirrup iron on that side and increasing it on the other. Leaning the body over has no effect whatsoever, for the weight of the rider tells only at the points of contact no matter at what angle the body may be to those points. If we watch a maestro employing the body aids the movement is barely perceptible.

Now we must consider the action of the REINS as AIDS. By means of the bit working on the tongue and bars of the mouth, they act on the head, neck and shoulders. The rider can thus regulate the position of the head in relation to the neck, the neck to the shoulders and the shoulders to the hind quarters. They can assist the legs by influencing the shoulders to assume a position which makes the hind quarters change direction.

The Five Reins. This classification is of comparatively recent evolution. It came from Weedon. Although these methods of rein employment in various permutations and combinations have been employed by all good horsemen throughout the ages, they were not universally understood or appreciated.

It was rather amusing, almost pathetic, to find the FIVE REINS hailed as a new discovery by quite a number of people, mostly of the younger generation. These aids were certainly known to Xenophon, and Alexander the Great undoubtedly used them on Bucephalus.

A clear and simple explanation will dispel any confusion in the minds of those who are seeking enlightenment on the subject. Questions about these aids were not infrequent in I. of H. examinations and will probably appear in papers set these days.

Let us consider the respective employment of these different "Reins" and the result of their actuation on the horse. In practice they would, of course, be used in conjunction with the leg aids, but for the purpose of explaining the theory we will deal with the reins alone.

There is only lateral tension used with direct and indirect reins. A backward tension is exerted with reins of opposition.

(1) *Direct Rein.* This is simply the feel of the rein on one side or the other of the horse's mouth, so turning the horse's head in the required direction. By increasing the tension and so bringing the head further round, the weight of the head and neck, which is considerable, is obviously thrown on to the shoulder. The horse is thus off his balance. Suppose the Right Direct Rein is employed at the halt, the head turns to the right, bending the neck in a slight curve. Although he is off his balance, he is not allowed to move. This is the lateral flexion, an exercise most beneficial in keeping him good in the turns and preventing him from getting one-sided.

On the move, turning to the right. The Right Direct Rein is actuated at the exact instant that the off fore is about to leave the ground, the tension must be relaxed as the foot comes to earth. The result is that the horse's head is brought round out of the line of progression; he is off his balance; instinctively he works to regain it. Therefore, the off fore turns to the right and the near fore conforms, the hind quarters follow but are controlled by the legs. To keep on turning, tension must be exerted on the Direct Rein, each time the off fore foot is just going to leave the ground, and relaxed as it is about to land. It is not necessary to carry the hand far out when employing the Direct Rein, unless the horse is very obstinate or one-sided. Force should not be employed; the flexions of the wrist should be sufficient. The head, in truth, is coaxed round.

(2) *The Indirect Rein* is employed on the opposite side to the Direct Rein. At the halt to restrain forward movement, on the move to regulate the pace. Secondly, both at the halt and on the move, when the Direct Rein is in operation, this rein should be pressed slightly against the neck. This inculcates "Rein on the Neck". This neck pressure must not be continuous, but must be synchronized exactly with the action of the Direct Rein. On no account should the hands be passed across the withers and raised, otherwise the unhappy horse is asked to turn his head one way with the Direct Rein, while the Indirect Rein is pulling in the other direction.

This rein is employed when riding with one hand, particularly at Polo, but the horse or pony must be bridle wise and the feel on the reins must be synchronized with the movement. A good illustration of the proper employment of these two reins is to be seen when a really good jockey coaxes an awkward horse round a bend.

(3) *The Direct Rein of Opposition.* This term may at first sight sound confusing, but after examination, it will be found quite simple. The term Opposition is used to indicate that a force or aid is brought into play, to produce a movement opposite to some

extent to that initiated by the application of the Direct Rein, and further to assist the leg aids to govern the hind quarters.

To actuate this Rein, say on the offside, the right hand, having acted direct as per (1), is then drawn back, kept low and inward, with the rein even touching the off side of the neck, so that, while the head is turned to the right, it is brought back a trifle and slightly raised, thus shifting some of the weight of the head and neck on to the shoulder. Again the question of re-adjustment of balance arises, and for this purpose the horse is inclined to move his hindquarters over to the left, unless the rider's legs order otherwise. This Rein has also a reining back action, it is most useful in the turn, at the halt it is used to turn a horse on the forehand or on his centre, in conjunction of course with the leg aids.

On the move, it is not quite so useful, unless it is necessary to restrain the horse, as it reduces the stride of the foreleg on the side applied and tends to turn a horse on his forehand by swinging his hind-quarters out. Perhaps the best illustration of the usefulness of this Rein, is in the case of a horse trying to shy, or look at something, say on the left side of the road. The novice pulls the horse's head round, probably with no light hand, towards the suspicious object. The hind quarters fly out into the road. The more a horse looks at it, the less he likes it. The result can be imagined. Now the workman makes a very different showing: anticipating that his mount is likely to shy, he gently brings the Direct Rein into play, so turning the head ever so little from the feared object, then almost immediately he switches on to this rein. While keeping the head thus slightly turned to the right, he puts some of the weight and neck on the right shoulder. Any tendency to accelerate is checked by both Reins and the right leg is put on, to keep the hind quarters from swinging out. Naturally the left REIN must be all this time in nice contact. This Rein is much in use in the passage, etc., as will be seen later. At the halt, the horse will turn right on centre or forehand. On the move, the stride of the off fore will be shortened and the horse will turn sharp right.

(4) *Indirect Rein of Opposition in front of the Withers.* This is simply the Indirect Rein applied with rather more feeling, with the hand very slightly raised and in front of the withers. It is mostly of service in the turns, passage and restraint and tends to shift some of the weight of the head and neck on to the opposite shoulder. When turning at the halt, this Rein brings a horse short round, it has a reining back action and helps to get a horse back on his hocks; also to bring the forehand round, so effecting a turn on the centre or haunches, again with the assistance of the leg aids. It is much used in training polo ponies to turn. First the Direct Rein is applied, immediately followed by the Indirect Rein. To teach neck pressure, then, on goes this rein to get him back on his hock, or to turn him on the centre,

according to the pressure, and round he goes. The legs, of course, have a good deal to say. This rein is also most useful in "changing legs".

(5) *Indirect Rein of Opposition behind the Withers.* This rein is of great utility, as it acts, not only on the forehand, but also is important in the control of the hind quarters, thus it is a most useful partner to the leg.

The hand must be kept well down and drawn well back. A good feel exerted on the mouth, rein pressed against the neck, but feel and neck pressure must be synchronized with the horse's movement. This Rein, applied on the offside, will induce movement of both forehand and hind quarters, over to the left. Most useful in the passage.

N.B. In the application of the FIVE REINS. When one Rein is not employed it must not be thrown loose, but a nice light contact must be maintained, as that Rein may be required at very short notice; if loose and taken up suddenly there will probably be a jerk.

The best way to get a good understanding of the use and application of the FIVE REINS is first to apply them at the halt and then on the move, noting carefully and exactly the reaction of the mount. Later on, you will be able to make certain combinations as required, although, where only one side is mentioned, naturally the Reins can be applied to both sides.

CHAPTER VII

_____

THE FUNDAMENTAL PRINCIPLE

Now I come to what I submit is the FUNDAMENTAL PRINCIPLE OF HORSEMANSHIP.

THROW A HORSE OFF HIS BALANCE SO THAT, IN RECOVERING IT NATURALLY, HE WILL DO WHAT YOU WANT HIM TO DO.

I propose to deal with this by stages, starting with the simplest case. Get someone to walk behind you with a hand on each shoulder. Walk along and as your right foot begins to go forward, let him turn your shoulders slightly to the right. Instinctively your foot points to the right, you turn in that direction, right foot comes to earth, left foot conforms. Why? *You were thrown off your balance; to regain it you had to turn to the right.*

Place your left leg over to the right in front of right leg. Now you are off your balance. If you do not allow the left leg to come back to the left side to regain your balance, you must move your right leg over to the right.

You are a biped, with a quadruped the effect is even greater.

As the horse walks along, actuate the DIRECT RIGHT REIN just as his off fore is coming forward,

77

thus so turning his head to the right. He is off his balance; the off fore turns to the right and comes to earth; he is now still more off his balance. The near fore turns right and conforms, but he is still off his balance; the hind quarters move over to the left and he is straight again.

To pass off to the right, you turn his head ever so slightly to the right with the RIGHT DIRECT REIN. Then a bit of left INDIRECT REIN OF OPPOSITION is put on, not sufficient to turn his head to the left, but enough to lighten the near shoulder and to cause him to move his near fore across and in front of his off fore; at the same time shifting the rider's weight over to the right, thus taking more weight off the near fore and the near hind. At the same time as the rider's left leg is applied, the horse's near hind is pushed across to the right in front of the off hind. The horse is now thoroughly off his balance; to regain it, he must either bring his near fore and near hind back, but this the rider prevents by the rein and left leg, or the horse must move the off fore and off hind over to the right, so that he is once more on balance, helped by the rider, taking the weight off the off side by rein and body.

In the same way in reining back, the rider, by over collecting, brings the centre of gravity as far back as possible. Assume that the rider wishes the near fore to start the rearward movement; the near fore is lightened by the INDIRECT REIN and by shifting the body over to the right, as soon as the near fore makes the backward step, the horse is off his balance; to regain it, the off hind must take a backward pace. Forward movement is of course prevented by both reins. The off fore and the near hind follow suit and rearward movement continues, until the rider brings the horse back to the usual position.

Application of the Aids. Having got a good appreciation of the rudimentary functions of the Aids, it now only remains to employ them correctly.

In dealing with the following movements, to make for simplicity, the Aids to be employed will be given in sequence, but it must be realized that in practice they have to be applied in rapid succession, practically simultaneously in some cases.

In all the following exercises, each step or movement must be deliberate and separate from the next, but always smoothly continuous and cadenced. It is a good plan, particularly for the novice, to count 1-2-3-4 as in music to get the rhythm. The moment an Aid has been answered, it must be taken off, to be re-applied, or another put on to produce the desired effect.

After each exercise, it is as well to relax, to sit easy with a loose rein, when a pat on the neck, a kindly word and a titbit may be given from time to time. An immediate award will be appreciated and make for complete understanding.

Balance. I think it is generally agreed that the primary function of the Aids is to produce BALANCE, but what is exactly understood by this term? It has often been laid down that a horse is balanced when his weight is evenly distributed on all four feet. Ever since I started—a good many years ago—to puzzle out equine problems, this definition has never quite satisfied me. When a horse is standing to attention, he will be better placed for movement if his forehand is light, the centre of gravity brought back as far as possible and the hind quarters ready for action. In this position the rider is sitting down, so helping to bring back the centre of gravity.

On the move, balance is a somewhat different matter and depends on the pace. Generally speaking, the weight should be so distributed that undue strain is never put on one particular leg as it meets the ground; when a fore and hind foot come to earth simultaneously, slightly more weight should be taken by the hind than the fore; it can stand it better. The hind feet should come as far forward as possible, and so gain the maximum mechanical advantage in the direction of propulsion. A well balanced horse may be defined as one with a light forehand, with hocks well under him, ready to accelerate instantly and go on all day without tiring just like a well-balanced athlete. Of course all horses are not naturally balanced—that is a matter of make and shape! But by schooling and good handling, a horse, not too well balanced by nature, can be vastly improved in this particular.

In racing, the idea is to get the jockey's weight as far forward as possible, so as to assist the hind quarters in propulsion. The light forehand does not apply in this case except at the start, when it is a treat to see a real artist bring his mount, beautifully balanced, to the tapes and off into his stride the moment they go up.

At the Halt. The preliminary exercises should be carried out at the halt; no exercise should be started unless a horse is standing balanced.

Standing collected or to attention, i.e. balanced.

(1) Apply both legs, not quite strongly enough to induce forward movement, but just enough to make him *want* to move.

(2) A split second later, feel both reins equally, raise horse's head and bring it back a trifle. The mouth should be level with the withers, the head bent at the poll, with the front of the face at an angle of about fifty degrees to sixty degrees with the vertical. The rein pressure brings the centre of gravity back. The legs make the horse reach for the bridle—*chercher la bride*. A dead pull must not be exerted, just a light give and take contact— inducing the horse to play with his bit. The hocks must be under him. A horse should not be kept too long in this position.

Usefulness. Balance, showing preparedness to move in any direction. "Standing out" is not a necessary accomplishment but can be practised if desired. In all the following exercises a start must be made with the horse collected.

Flexions (direct). Both reins felt, by action of third and fourth fingers and wrist if necessary, cause the horse to bend his head just behind the poll and yield to the pressure of the bit. The moment this is given, rein tension must be relaxed, thus teaching the horse that, when he yields to the bit, the pressure ceases, but contact must be maintained.

(Lateral). Application of the Direct Rein, say to the right, makes the horse flex his head to the right, from just behind the poll. There must not be a continuous strain on the reins, nor must it be jerky but little coaxing pulls. The Indirect Rein can be used gently against the neck. Flexing to the right, the left leg must be ready to prevent the hind quarters moving to the left. Again both legs keep the horse up to the bit and prevent reining back; three or four flexions to both sides are sufficient at a time. Although flexing is generally only carried out as above, I have always found it beneficial to coax the head round a bit more and get a gentle curve in the neck after a few flexions as above.

Usefulness. Keeps the horse's mouth fresh and neck suppled, prevents and cures hardness of mouth or one-sidedness. A first-class rider introduced to an unknown horse can sense immediately the sensitivity of the mouth, diagnose suitability of bit and consequently know how that particular horse should be handled. Moreover splendid practice for "hands" and a preliminary of all the following exercises.

Turns (Right Angle).

On the Forehand. i.e., Pivoting on the fore legs, turning say to the right.

(1) Right Direct Rein lightly flexes the head to the right, a little Right Indirect Rein of Opposition puts weight on the left shoulder, the left rein against the neck. If the horse is prevented from advancing by both reins and from reining back by both legs, he will move his off fore, just a bit to the right; the near fore will conform. If plenty of right leg is applied, his quarters will move round to the left. His natural inclination to preserve his balance assists the aids very considerably. A quarter right, a half right, a three-quarters right and a right about, should all be practised, similarly with (2) and (3).

(2) *On Centre.* The reins are applied very much in the same way as in (1). But the fore feet are made to move with a little more freedom, the turn being made as if pivoted on the centre of gravity. The hind legs move over naturally to the left to restore balance but can be assisted by the rider's right leg. The left leg is applied to restrict too much movement of the hind quarters.

(3) *On the Haunches.* In this case the pivot is on the hind quarters. The reins are applied in much the same way as in (1) only more so. The Indirect Rein of Opposition behind the withers may possibly have to be applied. The off fore must be made to take larger steps to the right, followed similarly by the near fore. At the same time the hind feet,

practically marking time, turn towards the right, thus preserving the horse's balance. The left leg must be ready to prevent the hind quarters swinging out to the left, each movement must be deliberate, rein and leg must be eased, as each movement of fore or hind leg is made, then put on again. This is most important.

Turns on the Move.

(1) *On the Forehand.* I do not recommend this turn when on the move. It is a strain on the forelegs and uncomfortable for the rider, while at fast paces the horse certainly feels as if he is going to topple over; in fact sometimes he does.

(2) *On Centre.* This is the best turn on the move, comfortable for the rider, and easy on the horse's legs. Say to the right at walk, trot, canter or gallop. As the off fore is just coming forward apply the Right Direct Rein; the head is just turned to the right, the horse is off his balance. The near fore will conform naturally, but can be assisted by the application of the Left Indirect Rein. He will try to adjust by swinging his quarters off to the left. The right leg may be used to assist this movement if necessary; the left leg must stand by, ready to check too much left movement by hind quarters, which would, if allowed, mean a turn on the forehand. A touch of Right Indirect Rein might be required to lighten the off shoulder, if the off fore doesn't come round readily. In effect, the hind feet will follow in the track of the fore feet. It is a very

good exercise to make this turn round a post or a mark on the ground in complete circles at varying distances from the centre.

(3) *On the Haunches.* Say to the right. No matter what the pace, that pace must be slightly checked by both Direct Reins, bringing the centre of gravity as far back as possible. The Right Direct is applied as the off fore is just coming forward, followed immediately by the Right Indirect Rein of Opposition, to lighten the off fore. At the same time the left Indirect Rein is pressed against the neck. As the head comes round to the right, the horse is off his balance. The near fore will conform and he will naturally swing his quarters off the left to regain balance and straighten up, but this tendency must be checked by strong application of the left leg. Consequently, to adjust balance, he must simply mark time with his hind feet, while turning them to the right to conform with the movement of his fore feet. It is evident that if this turn is accomplished at any pace, it brings considerable strain on the hind legs, especially the hocks. It should, therefore, not be employed, except when really necessary, as in polo, where and when a sudden change of direction becomes imperative. In all these turns, rein and leg application must be eased as soon as the desired movement has been achieved, but be put on immediately for the next step. At the canter and gallop it is essential that the leg on the side to which the turn is to be made should be leading.

Before making any turns, whether on the move or at the halt, *the horse must be balanced.* This is specially essential at the faster paces. Perfect synchronization must be aimed at, the reins actuated at the exact moment the leading foot is just coming forward and relaxed as it comes to earth, to be put on again in the same manner.

The importance and usefulness of these turns are self-evident. These turns have been made to the right: if required to the left, read left for right leg or rein.

As we have been dealing with schooled horses, the body aids have not been considered necessary, but when a horse is "sticky" it is advisable to lighten whichever leg it is required to move by shifting the weight of the body to the opposite side.

To Rein Back. Any length of pace (in reason) can be produced by duration of the tension of the reins and application of the legs. Horse standing square. Determine how many paces and which leg is to start off, say four paces. Near fore to start. (1) Feel both reins lightly, then employ left Indirect Rein of Opposition in front or behind the withers. The weight should be shifted to the right, this further lightens the near shoulder and makes it easier for the horse to lift his near fore; tension on both reins lightens forehand, if necessary shift the weight back a trifle in the saddle, but do not lean back. The right leg must be ready to prevent the hind quarters pushing out to the right.

86

(2) Simultaneously relax leg pressure. The near fore comes back a pace, the off hind conforms to regain balance; the moment the near fore comes back the required distance, ease rein tension and close the legs.

(3) Again feel both reins, employ Right Indirect Rein of Opposition to lighten off shoulder, at the same time shift rider's weight to the left. This brings back the off fore and the near hind will conform to regain balance. The left leg must be ready to prevent the hind quarters pushing out to the left, because of the Right Indirect Rein of Opposition.

(4) Relax leg and rein pressure as in figure (2), repeat (1), (2), (3) and (4) for the fourth pace; bring the off fore level with the near fore, close legs and stand still. The rein back must be quite straight, both legs must be ready to prevent quarters swinging out and the reins equally must govern the forehand. Eight paces should be the maximum; vary from two to eight. Always count.

Back and Forward. Say three paces each way, beginning with off fore. Then rein back as above.

After three paces back. (1) Just as the off fore comes to the ground at the end of the third pace, squeeze with both legs, ease both reins and say "*Forward*"; this will make it move forward; (2) as it is about to come to the ground, feel both reins, relax leg pressure.

(3) Squeeze both legs, ease both reins, thus sending the near fore forward.

(4) Repeat (2).

(5) Squeeze both legs, ease both reins, thus sending the off fore forward. Make it come down level with the near fore, by feeling both reins.

(6) Halt at attention.

It is best in this exercise, to do an odd number of paces, say figures (1) and (5), so as to finish with one fore leg behind the other so that the back leg lands, pauses, then goes forward keeping time with the counting. Figures 1-2-3—1-2-3.

Usefulness. A horse should rein back easily and smoothly with his head in the correct position. Absolutely necessary for opening gates, pulling back tail to hedge for "hounds, please", keeping the mouth easy. It is good training for muscles and is the first step towards reduction of speed and collection on the move. The forward movement inculcates propulsion. For the rider it provides most useful practice in rein, leg and body aids, which should hardly be perceptible to the onlooker.

To Move Forward. No matter at what pace, there must be no jerk and, above all, no jiggling with the legs and niggling with the reins; some riders positively force their horses to rear by such handling. The rider must never be left behind for this will most certainly mean a jab at the horse's mouth.

A horse standing properly to attention should

move off into any pace, simply by the application of the correct leg aids and a split second later the required amount of rein ease. For the sake of both horse and rider this exercise should be constantly practised, from the halt into the walk, trot and canter.

The horse, being a creature of habit, will soon recognize and obey the leg aids in accordance with the force employed. Particularly with young horses, the voice will materially assist, they will even hear a whisper. Go on, walk on, trot (sharp and short), canter (also short).

Except for polo ponies and race-horses under the gate, it is never advisable to train for anything faster than the canter from the halt.

Usefulness. Is too obvious.

Increasing and Decreasing Speed. Which is the same thing as lengthening and shortening strides. A careful study of instantaneous photographs shows that, even when a horse is all out, he cannot put his fore feet further forward than a vertical line drawn through the front of the nose (Plate III); this does not apply to Show Hackneys. It stands to reason that if the head is brought back, i.e., flexed, the length of the stride is automatically shortened and speed consequently reduced.

The direct flexions and reining back provide the first steps towards control, without which the rider is simply a passenger. These exercises, which are so beneficial to the rider, also impress on the horse that the best, simplest and easiest way for him to relieve the bit pressure on his mouth and tongue is to yield, i.e., give his head and lower jaw. At the same time the rider must stick to his part of the bargain by easing the rein pressure at the psychological moment as a just reward.

The Passage or Pass. This is a most useful exercise for both rider and horse. When completely understood and mastered it can be claimed that, for all ordinary purposes, the education of man and beast is complete. It simply means that the rider can apply the aids correctly and thus has complete control, because the horse acts and is obedient to the aids.

The passage is just the lateral movement to the right or to the left, either at right angles or diagonally to the line of advance. Beginners should be initiated on a well-trained horse, in school or *manège*, starting with the horse's head towards a wall or enclosure, in which case the passage or pass will be in the direction of the line of advance. The reason for recommending this first step, is that the novice is not bothered with restraint or regulation of forward movement and can thus concentrate on the perfection of the aids for the sideways movement. As soon as these aids are mastered, the passage should be executed across the school or *manège*, always from some post or mark to another.

Right Pass. With left shoulder out.

(1) The horse must be placed facing the wall or enclosure just clear of it and at an angle of about 45° to 30° to it.

(2) To produce the required sidelong movement the near fore and near hind must pass to right and come to earth in front of the off fore and off hind respectively. The following aids are applied simultaneously.

(*a*) Right Direct Rein; just sufficient to turn the head very slightly to the right; this throws the horse a little off his balance, but not enough to make him want to move his off fore.

(*b*) Shift the rider's weight to the right; this lightens the near fore and near hind and makes it easier to lift and move these legs, at the same time as putting the horse off his balance.

(*c*) Left Direct Rein of Opposition, generally behind the withers. This puts the weight on the off shoulder, further lightening the near shoulder.

This rein certainly induces the near fore to move over to the right; but the fact that the rider's weight has been shifted to the right and the off shoulder "weighted" means that the horse is thrown off his balance and to regain it he moves his near fore and then his off fore to the right. He is unlikely to move his off fore first, that leg being weighted; but in case he should try, the Right Direct Rein of Opposition must be brought into operation.

(*d*) Left leg applied just behind the girth, which

helps the near hind over to the right and is the natural movement in the effort to regain balance. The right leg is used if necessary to keep him up to his bit, prevent reining back or hurried movement to the right.

As soon as the near fore and near hind have responded the horse is definitely off balance. The aids are taken off, leaving the off fore and off hind to move to the right as they must naturally do to regain balance. At the same time the left rein and left leg must be ready to prevent the horse attempting to regain his balance by bringing the near fore and near hind back to the left.

As soon as the off fore and hind have come to rest, (a), (b), (c) and (d) are again applied, taken off and so on.

The original angle of about 30° to 45° must be maintained. If the horse tries to get "square to the boards", i.e., at right angles to the track, application of the Right Direct Rein of Opposition and the right leg will check him. If, on the other hand, he tries to reduce the angle, the Left Direct Rein of Opposition and the left leg will bring him back to the correct position.

The above movements should be smooth and regular. 1-2-3 and 4, etc., near fore and hind moving to the odd numbers, off fore and hind to the even numbers.

The more imperceptible the application of the aids, the better the performance. Niggling with the leg, as is too often seen, is indicative of inefficiency, as also is "head to the left"; it must be slightly turned in the direction of movement.

It is not necessary to pass all round the school. Eight, ten or twelve steps are sufficient; then halt, straighten the horse's head and neck with the Left Direct Rein. Sit easy. Then go on again.

When all goes well, right shoulder in should be made. The horse having been facing the boundary wall or fence at the given angle, to bring his right shoulder in, i.e., towards the centre of the school, he must be turned to the right on his centre, as at the halt, and placed with his hind feet just inside the track, the body at an angle of 30° to 45° with the side of the school.

Left Pass. Exactly the same aids as for right pass, except for left read right. But as there is no barrier to prevent forward movement, both reins must be used for restraint if necessary.

The next movement should be the passage across the school. First straight across, i.e., at right angles to the boards; aids as for right or left pass.

Then diagonally, usually known as the half-pass or half-passage, but quarter and three-quarter should also be undertaken as already indicated, aiming to arrive at the other side of the school exactly on a given mark.

For the full passage, say to the right, the near hind and near fore must pass straight over to the right in a line at right angles to the boards. In the oblique passage these feet move across, but at the same time advance a trifle according to the degree of obliquity required, so as to arrive exactly on the mark aimed at. The aids are exactly as required for the full passage, but in addition, as each odd number step is taken there must be a slight easing of both reins and impulsion imparted by both legs which sends the horse's fore and hind foot (odd number leg) forward a few inches, which will produce the oblique movement. The "even number" leg will conform naturally.

At the Trot Right Pass. The horse must be brought to the taking off mark at an absolutely collected trot when the aids are applied for the Right Pass, except that the first essential is to place him 30° to 45° to the boards. The Right Direct Rein and the Left Indirect Rein of Opposition behind the withers plus fairly strong application of the left leg, to push his quarters over to the right, will do the trick. There should be no pause nor hesitation. At the offset it will be sufficient to produce a very oblique movement, say three-quarters, but as efficiency and perfect synchronization are attained, a full pass should be accomplished.

This should suffice for all ordinary practical purposes.

Usefulness. A few examples will indicate the benefit derived from complete mastery of the passage Aids. To begin with, it is impossible to open or shut a gate unless you can pass a horse over to the right or left, rein him back, turn on the forehand or haunches.

What strange evolutions and yanking at mouths are to be seen out hunting, even at Hunters Trials and at Gymkhanas.

At the risk of repetition let us suppose that a horse shies or is going to shy or looks at something on the near side of the road. The inexperienced rider hauls the head round to the left with loud and pointed remarks, too often emphasized with the stick. This produces a crablike movement well into or across the road, or at best it is only the quarters; he is lucky if a following car misses him. The "workman" quietly but firmly applies the aids for the left pass. If he says anything, it's in the direction of "Silly ass—there is nothing to hurt you", or soothing words to that effect. What is the result? The horse, wanting to get away from the offending object, attempts to move to the right, which practically amounts to a right pass, full or oblique. The rider, applying the aids for the left pass, except that instead of the Left Direct Rein, the Right Direct Rein of Opposition behind the wither is applied, brings the head away from the alarming point, lightens the off shoulder and pushes the forehand over to the left. There are then two forces in action: the horse's to the right, the aids to the left. If these are equal, the result is a straight line. If the horse exerts the stronger force, at the worst it is only a slight deviation from the straight, and the direction is speedily rectified. A kindly word or two and a pat on the neck and the trouble is soon over.

If time permits and the locale is suitable, a few turns up and down past the offending object, with the aids properly applied, will prove a useful lesson.

It is extraordinary how so many riders are unable to steer a horse in a straight line direct on any given object. I have witnessed many weirdly serpentine movements for the reason that the riders relied entirely on the Direct Rein. Whereas if the horse is inclined to the right, had they applied the aids for the left pass, combined with the leg aids, all would have been well. Get into a field, fix some distant object like a tree, stack, or house. Trot straight to it. Get someone to stand behind in line with you and the object. Get a report on your line of advance, then try it at the canter and finally the gallop. You'll be surprised. This applies very strongly in racing. We hear a great deal nowadays of swerving and consequent interferences, whereas, when jockeys had "a leg each side" and could apply the rein and leg aids, horses ran a deal straighter on the course. When riding off at polo the passage "Aids" are invariably employed.

Lastly, but by no means of least importance, comes the matter of keeping a horse in at his fences. If a horse is trying to "get out", it's not much use and most unworkmanlike to haul his head round. He will almost certainly "give you his head" and push his body off in the opposite direction. But if he is trying to get out to the left and the rider applies the aids for the right pass with plenty of Left Indirect Rein of Opposition behind the withers and a very strong left leg, even if the horse is not responsive to the aids, he is a very resolute brute if he does get out. At the same time should he try to turn round to the left, the right leg must prevent his hind quarters going to the right. Such a horse should be put through the school and taught to passage; having learnt his lesson, any good horse-man will be able to keep him straight.

Many more examples could be advanced, but the above should clinch the argument.

Changing the Leg at the Canter. Before proceeding to the application of the aids necessary for this evolution, it is advisable to watch carefully the consecutive movements of the horse's fore and hind legs. Study photographs and cine photos. You will thus get the true sequence.

To Change from the off fore leading to near fore leading. (1) Determine exactly when and where the change is to be made, and before reaching that spot say two strides away, exert a little pressure on both reins to lighten the forehand, get the horse back on his hocks and even reduce his pace slightly. Give a trifle of Right Direct Rein to flex his head the least bit to the right, but without turning him in that direction.

(2) The instant the off fore touches earth and the

near fore is *about* to come forward, apply the Left Direct Rein, immediately followed by the Left Indirect Rein of Opposition, to throw the weight still more on the off fore and off hind. The Left Direct Rein will turn the horse's head to the left, throwing him off his balance; in order to regain same, he must push out the near fore. Passing the rider's weight over to the right makes it easier for him to do so and should suffice to make the near fore lead. The hind legs naturally follow. But to assist further the Left Indirect Rein of Opposition is put on. As the near fore is coming forward impulsion should be exerted by both legs, with the necessary easing of both reins. The right leg should be applied and the left leg should be ready to prevent the hind quarters throwing off to the left. A slight neck pressure with the off rein is recommended.

(3) It is essential that the hind legs should exactly conform to the movement of the fore legs. If not, the horse will be cantering disunited, an uncomfortable thing for both rider and horse. In this case the horse should be changed back to off fore leading and again changed to near fore leading. Or else pulled up to a trot or walk and started again on the near fore.

The Change from near to off. Simply reverse right and left.

Once a rider and horse can change correctly on the turns it is not a difficult matter to change on the straight. Three strides off fore leading, three strides near fore leading and so on, is a fine exercise for both. The same aids are applied except that, say changing from off to near the Left Direct Rein is not used to bring the horse round, but only to flex the head slightly to the left, while the Rein in Opposition is used more strongly to put weight on the off fore and lighten the near fore shoulder. The legs, in addition to the aids (*vide* (2)), are used to keep the horse straight.

It shows very bad handling if, when changing off to near fore, the horse's head is seen to be round to the right. It must definitely be flexed towards the side of change.

Sometimes a horse will try to change back. A rider must watch for this; to prevent it, he should keep on the aids which made him change, to a mild degree. If he changes without orders, change him back on the straight if possible; if not, on the turn, or at the next corner. In changing, there must be no acrobatic contortions when shifting weight, no waving of arms or flapping of legs.

Many horses appear to have a favourite leg, in that they prefer to canter or gallop with one fore leg leading in preference to the other. Unless this is due to unsoundness a horse should be made to change on to the other leg and be kept on it, until he uses both legs indiscriminately.

Usefulness. Is a matter of Safety First. It is obvious that if a horse is cantering or galloping, with the near fore leading and turns or is turned to the right, without changing on to the off fore leading, he is very liable to cross his legs, which generally means a real purler; if he avoids a fall he is almost certain to hit himself, and anyhow it will not mean a nice handy turn. Racing, he is bound to go wide, while definitely he is off his balance. Even in the school or *manège*, I have seen horses cross their legs and fall at a corner when cantering on the wrong leg. On the right rein, i.e., going round to the right, the off fore must lead and vice versa.

A thorough knowledge of the Aids for the change will prevent a horse changing when galloping, which is so often seen on the training gallops and even on the race-course, when lads or jockeys yank and yaw instead of sitting still and using the correct rein Aids. When changing under these conditions a horse will often hit himself and invariably loses ground. On say a left-hand course, it is quite possible to make a horse strike off with the near fore leading, or if not, to change him early in the race and keep him so all the way. He will round the bend cleverly, and probably gain a length or two.

At polo changing is of utmost importance. Players must be able to apply all the necessary aids with one hand. A properly schooled pony will change and turn on a soup plate, if he is steadied, the body aids applied and the indirect rein pressed against his neck. It is a mistake to think that all this is academic or high faluting. It is of great practical importance.

It is a liberal education to watch real artists competing in a dressage test and to note how they apply the aids practically imperceptibly.

CHAPTER VIII

AN APPRECIATION OF THE AIDS

I HAVE been fortunate to have many friends who were superb horsemen. But very few of them, except those who were soldiers, would ever admit there was any advantage in schooling either horse or rider. The fact is that they had ridden from baby-hood, had learnt the leg aids in the nursery and solved the problem of the Five Reins as, or more, easily than learning the multiplication table, and were unaware that they had done so.

I remember staying with a friend, a Master of Hounds, a really fine horseman. At dinner I had spoken in favour of schooling and the Aids but he, and some of his guests, refused to take me seriously.

Next morning, a non-hunting day, we went out on some young horses. My friend was riding a four-year-old. Soon after we got out of the park gates, this four-year-old tried to shy at a heap of stones by the roadside. My friend, at once and automatically, applied the correct Aids. After which he walked the horse past the heap of stones until it had ceased even to notice that there was anything there.

We then came to a gate. My friend, uncon-sciously using the correct aids, opened it. After that we came to a small hedge. The four-year-old tried to refuse. My friend brought the Five Reins into play at the psychological moment; timed the leg aids perfectly, the stride was lengthened, the office, as it is called, given at the exact time and place; the four-year-old took off and jumped perfectly. Throughout that morning, my friend all unknowingly gave a perfect display of the finished use of the Aids.

On our way home I told him so.

"Oh. Any damn fool can do it," he replied.

I think that many critics of schooling of horse and rider are like my friend. Experts who have assimilated from childhood all the teaching which this and other books contained. But, except for those fortunate few, schooling, if anything like perfection is aimed at and for branches of equitation like hunting, polo, show jumping, is imperative. And if you want to break, make or re-break horses you must obviously be highly proficient.

In September, as soon as we returned from manoeuvres, I used to bring up my hunters which had been turned out. And into the school they went. It freshened up their mouths and mended their manners, particularly if they had been raced or point-to-pointed. It made them fit more quickly than by ordinary exercise; for the school exercises are to a horse what physical training is to the human; one could see the muscle coming up and feel it hardening.

I used to get the polo ponies up, as early as I

could in February or March if possible, and school them in the same way. It did them no end of good and kept my hand in.

Young horses I bought, with the hope of getting a race out of them, did a three months' course, which improved their galloping and jumping to a very marked degree, muscled them and made them put on weight. A horse well balanced and collected must gallop better and jump off his hocks with less effort than one which has not had the benefit of a thorough school training.

Schools and *manèges* were pretty fully occupied in working hours in barracks, which left the early morning, lunch-time or afternoon for private tuition. But it was well worth it. I mentioned this, as so many people complain that they haven't time! Yet much can be done towards mastering and inculcating the Aids during an ordinary hack ride.

I have had many arguments with people who assert that race-horses are balanced and can gallop, though they have never been taught the Aids. The examples which these opponents of the Aids put forward are invariably horses of perfect make and shape, with beautiful natural balance, invariably high-priced yearlings, picked out by superlative judges of the ideal racing mechanism. Moreover, they are handled in their races by jockeys who can hold them together and preserve their natural balance. But there is a very large percentage of horses, not so well favoured by nature, that would do better and probably win races if they had been schooled and taught the Aids, which would have corrected any deficiency of balance.

Some critics assert that application of the Aids gets the horse over-collected and thus cramps his movements. I suspect that this criticism arises out of the critics' own unhappy experiences, because, to produce over-collection, the Aids must have been misunderstood and wrongly applied. Over-collection means that a horse's neck is severely arched, the whole head brought back, with the front of the face vertical. A consideration of the two preceding chapters will prove that none of the Aids properly applied produces this unpleasant state of affairs. Consider a high-class polo pony, an animal schooled and trained to the last degree, yet one of the fastest, handiest and most active creatures on four legs. If he were over-collected he would be useless.

It is possible to cite many examples, illustrating the practical advantage obtaining from the Aids. Let two suffice.

(1) Siegfried Sassoon in the *Memoirs of a Fox-hunting Man* tells how, in his first point-to-point, one of the competitors, whom he calls Boots Brownrigg, rounded a flag so closely that his foot must have touched it, whilst Sassoon himself went wide and lost many lengths. The hunt, though Sassoon does not say so, was the Southdown, and Boots Brownrigg was I, the author of this book. The reason why my foot nearly touched the flag, was not a matter of luck. The course was right-handed: I had my horse with the off fore leading; round

went my horse and I turned him a little behind the centre but not on his hocks; Right Direct Rein, Right Indirect slightly in opposition, left leg on, but right leg ready to push the hind quarters over to the left to make the turn less on the haunches. The Aids. My mount understood them; I understood and I applied them. And we scored!

(2) Hounds running left of and parallel to a grass lane down which three of us were galloping. Hounds turned left-handed, there was wire on our left, but an open gate came into view.

The other two shot on some distance past it, had to pull up and come back to it, thereby losing a lot of ground. My horse had off fore leading; I reduced pace and changed on to the near fore, turned on the centre and slipped through the gate. A man coming behind, said to me afterwards, "Extraordinarily handy horse that of yours." The horse was no more handy than his by nature. But, he had been schooled. He knew the Aids! And so did I!

The many who scoff at schooling and the Aids belong to what is known as the "In, over or through Brigade"; they are interested only in getting there and are indifferent as how best to get there. This obstinacy of theirs spoils many a good horse and though they know it not, deprives them of the great joy in a perfect ride. But they are getting fewer. The great present-day interest in dressage tests, Best trained Hack Class and Show Jumping is proof that people are getting Aid-Conscious.

AN APPRECIATION OF THE AIDS

After the introduction of gunpowder, light armour came into vogue. Therefore a lighter and handier horse became necessary. Doubtless something was learnt from the Saracens in the Holy Wars. Anyway, it became evident that the mounted man's life depended largely on the handiness of his horse. For this reason Dressage and the Aids came to be evolved. Thus the *Haute Ecole* came into being. In all countries there was a large number of riding schools, where dressage was constantly practised. It is—I am old enough to regret it—no longer necessary for the Army to know anything about the Aids, but the place of the cavalry and artillery— exponents of the art—is taken by many gifted and hard working amateurs, amongst whom of course are a certain number of Army officers.

Haute Ecole does not quite come within the scope of this book, except of course the initial stage which applies to every variety of horsemanship. *Haute Ecole* is a highly specialized art and no man and horse can ever reach the heights unless they belong exclusively to each other—the horse must be yours and yours alone.

If I were a trainer, I would most certainly start my apprentices and young lads by teaching them the utility seat, hands, the Aids and how to use them. When proficient, I would get their knees up by degrees until the chasing or flat racing seat was reached. I am certain that a course on these lines would be highly beneficial to the pupils and would be appreciated by the horses in training.

CHAPTER IX

HANDS

(1) WE have reached now, what is, in my opinion, the most important Essential of Horsemanship. The subject of Hands has been discussed and debated for many, many years. I have heard it asserted times without number, that Hands are born and not made. I have never subscribed to that opinion. Provided that a rider is not brutal by nature, possesses a fair amount of intelligence, sympathy and sensitivity, he or she can easily acquire good hands by careful study, practice and the determination to succeed. As already explained, good hands cannot be hoped for until the seat is firm.

Now please help me to prove my point. Learners are invariably told, "Don't take a dead hold, pull and ease, ease and pull", but I have never been told, nor heard it said, nor read, just when one must ease or just when one must pull. Being determined to improve my Hands, I devoted a lot of thought to this matter and came to the conclusion that the answer lay in synchronization of rein action and the horse's leg action.

For a start begin dismounted. Stand on the near side, put the right hand over the horse's neck, then take the bit reins. I suggest a pelham off side right hand, near side left hand, between first finger and thumb. Feel the mouth gently. If it is a tall horse, both hands could of course be under the neck.

If the animal is very free, he will step out nicely, if not, it is as well to have someone to walk behind to keep him up to his bit. Let him walk along freely for a few paces, then, as each fore foot is *just* leaving the ground, actuate the reins, easing the moment the foot comes to earth, then reins again as the other foot leaves the ground, easing as it comes down. Carry on with this exercise. It will be found that you can almost make the horse mark time. The hind feet of course conform to the movements of the fore feet.

By easing and bringing pressure on the mouth, correctly synchronized, one can step out, go slow and regulate the pace as required. In that lies the whole secret of Hands.

It is not quite so easy at first when mounted. Begin at the walk, bend over and watch the movement, then actuate the reins as above, ease and keep the horse up to his bit with your legs. Rein contact must be maintained and there should be no jerk at the reins. No more rein pressure should be used than is absolutely necessary, the play of the wrist must be in action, like the top joint of a fishing rod. Practise this until you can make the horse walk at any pace you like. It is quite possible to make a horse walk lame. As, say, the off fore is leaving the ground, put on the rein pressure almost at once, bring it to earth then as the near fore starts forward, ease and put on both leg aids, this will produce a full pace with the near fore; same again and again. This demonstrates complete control of movement.

It is more difficult at the trot. Begin by looking down and work in the same way as at the walk.

At the canter it is a little easier than at the trot. Again start with looking down, working the reins as at the halt. After some practice, the rider will find that there is a certain feel which indicates exactly what the feet and legs are doing. Get down to six miles an hour, it is a delightful pace.

At the gallop the stride is longer, therefore the synchronization is easier to achieve. Very soon it will be found that, by sensing the movement of the forelegs, it will no longer be necessary to look down.

Study Plate III. If two race-horses are fully extended at a finish and you drop a perpendicular from each nose it will just about meet the extended fore foot. Examine every photo you see, watch horses galloping and you will find it is always the same. Now if by rein pressure you bring the head back, the fore foot does not make such a long stride, therefore the pace is reduced. Except in the case of high-stepping hackneys—an artificial gait— the fore foot cannot go further forward than a perpendicular from the nose. At full stretch the head is extended, the nose out as far as it can go.

Of course, some horses pull and need a fairly strong arm and wrist to obtain control, but easing

III. (a)   RACEHORSES FULLY EXTENDED AT ASCOT

(b) THE LANE: WEST SUSSEX SCHOOL OF EQUITATION

and pulling at the right moment will do the trick. How is it that with one rider, a horse is practically out of control, whereas with another he is fairly amenable? The answer is Hands. In all the application of the Aids, turns, reining back and so on, the principle is the same. Rein and leg Aids are brought into play as the movement requires, but eased the moment the movement is completed, to be put on again for the next movement. Not one fraction more of rein pull must be exerted than is sufficient to obtain the desired result.

The practical application of the above instructions will improve and make riding a joy to both the rider and the horse. The horse discovers sooner or later, if well handled, that as soon as he reduces pace, the pressure on the tongue and bars of the mouth ceases.

Now that not only horsemen but the general public are taking such a keen interest in dressage, show jumping and equitation generally, it is hoped that a higher standard of riding will result. At the shows and gymkhanas, we see really well trained hacks, generally beautifully handled. It is hoped the show ring will induce riding schools and livery stable proprietors to provide such hacks, but it is doubtful if they will jump to it, unless and until their customers are sufficiently proficient to ride them. Anyway, it is up to the riding school instructor to work in that direction.

There are quite a number of horses which have really hard mouths, particularly those who have

been raced a lot. While the well synchronized ease
and pull is just as essential the pull has to be a
really strong one. Particularly if the intention is to
ride chasing and point-to-pointing, which invariably means a snaffle. If the hands are kept in the
correct position, the muscle at the back of the
upper arm, the triceps, which is not much in
general use, will be brought into play. Therefore
it is necessary to work this muscle up, by means of
an elastic or weight and pulley exerciser.

CHAPTER X

JUMPING

JUMPING should not be attempted too early. How soon depends on the individual pupil. It is a great mistake to force it on, especially with the nervous type and with very young children who have not got the requisite strength of grip; moreover, many ponies jump a bit "strongly" and are not too easy to sit.

The horses and ponies for novices' jumping must be temperate and properly schooled so that they do not rush nor play up.

Nearly everyone wants to "try to jump", but apart from that natural and praiseworthy desire, jumping is really a great help towards perfection of grip and balance. The beginner should have the inevitable neck strap of course, but in addition a thin strap or strong string should be attached to the side of the stirrup iron next to the horse, so adjusted that it neither pulls the irons towards the horse nor lets them come away from the flanks; in fact it just allows them to remain in the natural position when the feet are in the irons. It must be explained that the rider is not being "tied on", that this arrangement simply prevents the feet from being poked forward, keeps the lower leg close and should the grip be loosened or the horse jump a bit too big and the rider be chucked up out of the saddle, the iron catches the instep. As the string or strap prevents the irons from rising, so is the foot kept down and the rider does not come off. The string or strap should be dispensed with as soon as the rider is sitting comfortably over about three feet.

By the time the rider has reached the jumping stage, he or she will be riding with reins. There is some diversity of opinion, as to whether the reins should be held in one hand or both when jumping. I strongly advise the latter method. Hunting, show jumping, schooling, and chasing, the reins should always be in both hands, therefore it is better to start as you mean to continue; besides it is easier to keep the hands down, as the spare hand will have a tendency to wave about. In the old sporting prints many of the riders have an arm raised above the head; the idea was that it helped to swing the body back before landing. This was termed "Hailing the cab" and is definitely not to be recommended. In the case of a fall, if an arm is free it is certain to shoot forward. With an arm so extended, there is every chance of a broken arm or wrist or a shoulder put out. Moreover, hands are invariably lighter with the reins in both hands. With the reins in the left hand, the right can of course take hold of the neck strap, but I have found that, provided that it is laid down as a hard and fast rule, the neck strap *must on no account be grasped until the horse is about to take off.* Grasping the neck strap at that moment with both hands, helps to inculcate the forward movement of the body and the downward and forward movement of the hands, at the same time giving the horse his head.

As a preliminary it should be explained that jumping is merely a glorified pace in the canter.

I propose to deal with this subject in phases, starting from zero for the beginner. It may be that there are some who recognize, or have had pointed out to them, their faults and shortcomings. It may not be necessary for those to start at phase 1. They should therefore concentrate on the phase or phases which will be of benefit to their special case.

What a lot of terribly bad jumping seats are still in evidence at our shows and gymkhanas as recorded by photographs in the daily and weekly press. Quite recently a winner was snapped with his face in his horse's mane, the body lying along the horse's back, the feet more than half way up the horse's flank. The most general fault is the lower leg almost horizontal and the foot drawn up and back. Contact is often lost and the body is all anyhow.

The danger is, specially with the young, that if they get into the money, thanks to the horse or pony, while riding really badly, they imagine they know all the answers and even resent criticism.

When I was running a school of equitation, I found it was a capital plan to use a ciné camera; when the film was projected on the screen the pupils could see for themselves what needed correction and attention. There was small need for my running commentary.

A couple of large mirrors on the walls of the school were also of great assistance.

I recommend a careful and detailed study of Plates III, IV, V and VI. In them one may see the perfection of seats over fences, demonstrated by great artists.

It may be that some may not need to spend much time on the preliminary phases and can pass along, but it is not wise to do so until each phase is really perfect.

Phase I should be devoted entirely to the SWING, i.e., the forward movement of the body just before the horse takes off, so that the student's weight is placed as far forward as possible, so as to relieve the hind quarters to the utmost at the moment of propulsion. It is essential that the mouth must not be interfered with, as the horse must of course raise his head. The rider's knee and lower leg must stay put.

The bar should, for a start, be just on the ground; the horse should walk, then trot and finally canter over it. The student must, just as the horse is about to take off, drop both hands on to the neck strap, swing the body forward and raise the seat off the saddle, from the knee, assisted a little by the stirrups. The swing should be practised when halted, trotting and cantering. The back must be slightly rounded; nothing looks so bad as a hollow back, with a stern, particularly a roomy one, sticking out behind. The elbows must be kept in. Very soon the bar may be raised to two feet and kept at that height until the swing is perfect and the student can sit nicely without stirrups and arms folded and *immer mit*. The bar should then be raised to three feet and the stirrup attachment dispensed with. The student must stay in this phase, until position and swing are really good. That will be plenty to think about.

Phase II. The student is now promoted to the *Grid*, a series of bars 1 ft. 6 ins. high, just sufficient distance apart to allow a horse or pony to jump in and out. The bars should not be fixed, but sufficiently heavy to give a horse a good rap if he hits. Students should be started with just two bars, stirrups, reins and neck straps; more bars are added, according to the size of the school or *manège*. If legs fly about, the stirrup attachment must be reintroduced. Very soon the student will be able to go the length of the grid, with arms folded, without stirrups and without assistance from the neck strap. When the grid can be negotiated perfectly, very important progress has been made. It means that the swing has been acquired and the student is not being left behind.

Phase III. The student may now be put to negotiate a three foot six fence, first with reins and stirrups, then without either. If all goes well, the double, then treble and then the lane, i.e., five fences, preferably wattle hurdles sloped (*see* Plate III). Great care must be taken not to make too heavy a call on the riding muscles. The instant a student feels them tiring, or the slightest strain, he must call a halt. When the end of this phase is reached, the seat, position and swing should be all that can be desired. It is a mistake to overload the student. We can now consider the higher science.

The first step is to make a careful study of the successive movements of a horse jumping loose, in the flesh, in photographs, or slow motion ciné. He approaches the fence head up. An instant before taking off the head is lowered just a trifle, then raised as his forehand rises and the hind quarters give the necessary propulsion to take him over. Rising, the head is still up and tucked in a trifle; as he tops the fence his body assumes the horizontal with the head a little advanced; as the descent begins, the head goes down and quarters go up, remaining so until the landing is accomplished. The head is then raised and the natural position of the canter or gallop is resumed. It must be realized that a horse's head and neck weigh a great deal and play a most important part in jumping in the matter of balancing; even the tail appears to assist.

Phase IV. It may be assumed that the inde-

IV. (a) MAJOR RODDICK ON KILSTAR. A marvellous performance illustrating *immer mit*
(*Sport and General Press Agency Ltd*)

(b) A. P. THOMSON. A bad peck
(*Kemsley Newspapers*)

(c) T. GRANTHAM ON MONAVEEN
(*Sport and General Press Agency Ltd*)

pendent seat has now been acquired, therefore the first step in this phase is to ensure that the student in no way interferes with or impedes the sequence of events. The secret is that, while a light contact is maintained, there must be no pull on the mouth. If the student misses the right moment for the swing, it is practically certain to mean a pull on the reins which entirely ruins the jump. The horse's head goes up, his mouth opens; he may get to the horizontal position, but will not be able to get his head down, consequently the hind quarters will not go up. If he hasn't hit with his forelegs he is absolutely certain to do so with his hind and will probably peck heavily and even fall. It also means that with head up and mouth open, he will make a cat-jump, back rounded and land badly on all four feet. This often occurs when a horse takes off too soon. One of the finest examples of *immer mit* that I have come across is exemplified in Plate IVA. Kilstar, at that time rather green, actually took off outside the wings and made a prodigious jump; Major Roddick, as can be seen, was not left behind, and did not yank at the reins; there was no interference. Result, Kilstar got over —a marvellous performance.

It is well, therefore, to devote this phase to the perfect timing of the swing, which can only be acquired by practice and concentration. The student must acquire that sensitivity which tells the brain that the horse is about to take off. Quick thinking will enable him or her to swing at the psychological moment, a split second before the actual take off. Then all will be well.

In addition to the *immer mit* the get back should be brought into play. This simply means that the instant the hind legs have cleared, the seat must be put back into the saddle (*see* Plates IV, V and VI). The two "Past Masters" demonstrate this to perfection. I have heard it stated that the object of getting back on landing is to reduce the weight on the forelegs. This, as Euclid used to say, is absurd. No matter how the weight of the rider is distributed, the total poundage of horse plus rider must all come on the forelegs on landing.

A horse always lands on one fore foot, instantly followed by the other; a moment later the hind feet come to earth. With the rider's seat back in the saddle, his weight is distributed between the seat, the knee grip and the stirrup bars.

But if the rider lands forward, his weight is entirely distributed between the knee grip and the stirrup bars, i.e., well forward. If he has the reins crossed, or his hands or any portion of the body are on the horse's neck, the weight is still more forward.

Therefore, under these conditions, should the horse peck, recovery is seriously impeded. The peck may easily be turned into a fall. Whereas, if the seat is on the saddle quite a proportion of the rider's weight is further back, which is obviously a very great assistance towards recovery. Every ounce tells.

JUMPING

A peck is due to hitting the fence, landing on an inequality or in soft ground, or to the horse being tired; or to an over-reach. The moment it happens there is considerable check and jar. If the rider is right forward, he is bound to go out on the horse's neck. If the lower leg is back and the feet up, he is pivoted about the knee with no lower leg grip; he is almost certain to come unstuck; if lucky he will land on the horse's neck. If he has his feet stuck out in front, again the lower leg grip is absent. The sudden check which a peck produces is bound to cause a thrust on the irons which tends to yank the knee out of position and the rider out of the saddle.

Under these three conditions it is self-evident that with so much weight forward the horse has a poor chance.

However, with the seat in the saddle and the lower leg in the correct position, when the peck comes, the rider will naturally be shot forward, but a quick thinker will assist matters by throwing the body backwards. In any case it is only a matter of a split second before the hind legs land to assist recovery, which is well on the way before the rider's weight comes forward to the points of knee grip and stirrup bars. Of course the hands must be pushed right forward. If necessary the reins should be allowed to slip, the horse must be given his head (*see* Plate IVb).

Pecks are rare in show jumping, but when they do occur, the riders do not always remain on top, for the good reason that they are not sitting correctly. The same thing happens in the case of a refusal.

In the case of a fall, ease the grip and tuck the head well down, chin on chest, round the back and land on the back of the shoulders. Schooling, hunting and in the show ring, hold on to the reins, but if the horse is coming over let go and roll clear. Chasing, let go the reins, lie still till the field has passed. A horse will avoid you unless you get up and move.

While I strongly advocate the seat back in the saddle as soon as the hind legs have cleared the fence, remaining so until the fore legs have landed (*see* Plates IV, V and VI), the seat must be raised off the saddle as the hind legs are landing, so as to ease the hind quarters and aid propulsion in the first get-a-way stride. The hands must be pushed forward, there must be no interference with the horse's mouth; the reins should only be slipped in the case of a peck. This may sound very difficult. It is of course the attainment of perfection which should be the aim and ambition of all riders.

In the event of a fall, one must get up and go on just as if nothing had happened. If incapacitated, it is imperative to ride the same horse as soon as possible. If a fence caused the upset, that fence, or one as like it as makes no difference, must be negotiated without delay. This procedure, if followed, is the sure way to promote and preserve nerve and control.

V. LT.-COL. HARRY LLEWELLYN, O.B.E., ON FOXHUNTER
(Sport and General Press Agency Ltd)

JUMPING

While on long leave, I had hacked down to the training stables. There was a short cut to the road which meant jumping three schooling fences, made up in the hedges. On this particular day it was raining and blowing hard. I was wearing a waterproof with a cape. The horse I was riding had been rather a confirmed refuser, but I had got him straightened out. Coming up to the first fence the cape blew over my head. What was I to do? I had to think quickly. If I pulled him out, he might revert to his evil ways, so I sat still and took a chance. It was dead easy; being blinded, I suppose, I was more sensitive. I felt him *prepare* to take off; I just swung and went with him. On my return to barracks, I proposed blindfold jumping to my special ride, but I did not meet with much enthusiasm until I was blindfolded and showed how easy it was. All was well then and the whole ride started this new game with enthusiasm.

I would therefore recommend all who really aim high to practise blindfold jumping. It's not necessary to be blindfolded, just shut your eyes tight as you approach the fence, but play fair. You will not get left behind if you practise this assiduously, because it improves your sensitivity and rapidity of thought and action.

It will have been noticed that from Phase I I have promoted the pupil to student.

By this time the student is really in a position to enter into the top class.

Phase V. What is known as the ZONE is that

spot at which a horse should take off in order to make a perfect jump. The distance from which the horse takes off should be one and a half times the height of the fence. The higher the fence, the more important it is to take off as near this point as possible.

It will be noticed that every time a horse takes off properly at the zone, it's odds on that he clears.

How then to bring a horse to the fence so that he takes off correctly?

No matter at what pace, the horse must be collected with his hocks well under him, otherwise he will be sprawling with the hocks away out behind and quite unable to bring the necessary propulsion into action. He may even dive into the fence off his forehand. But, if collected, with hocks and hind feet coming right forward as far as possible under his centre of gravity, the mechanical advantage is self-evident and spells maximum clearance with minimum exertion. *He must be made to jump straight.* It is quite possible to collect a horse without reducing his pace. Watch a really good jockey pull a tired horse together coming to the last fence and drive him at it. It is a sight worth seeing and a lesson to be assimilated.

Presentation. Firstly the horse must be presented, that is, he is moved towards the fence, always at right angles to it, never obliquely.

Slipping Point is a spot determined by eye and experience and varies considerably as to whether the subject is chasing, hunting, show jumping or schooling. Anyway, it is so many strides from the ZONE. For the sake of argument, let us make it five. The rider judges that five strides will take him over the zone and four will be short of it. Therefore he has to decide quickly how to adjust matters. He must either lengthen the stride, so that four will bring him just right, or shorten the stride, so that five will be the correct answer.

Chasing, the slipping point will be considerably further back; hunting, also but not quite so far. Chasing, the stride should always be lengthened. Hunting, I recommend lengthen if going fast, but shorten at slower pace. If you find that, in spite of your efforts, the horse is not coming right, you must not try to correct matters at the last moment, for any interference would be fatal. You must sit tight and go with him if he takes off too soon and give him his head. If he gets under the fence, prepare for a buck over; ease the reins and hope for the best; he often gets over if left alone.

There are some cunning old stagers that can measure their stroke, put in a short one or stand back. Leave it to them and don't interfere.

The lengthening of the stride should be done with the leg and easing the rein at the exact moment (*see* Hands). A slight application of the spur may be needed, but never the whip. The rider should sit still, calm and collected, no acro-

batics, riding a finish, or rowing the boat. To shout
HUP is quite uncalled for; the horse knows when to
take off. I have known it to provoke jeers from the
audience. I would again emphasize that in jumping, the whip should never be used.

The Office is a term used to denote the application of leg and perhaps the spur to indicate to the
horse when to take off, and to produce increased
propulsion, synchronized of course with an easing
of the reins. With a keen and willing horse the
office is simply a tightening of the lower leg grip.
It is evident that this application must be exactly
timed. If it is too early, it will upset the horse;
if too late, the horse will have taken off.

A nice contact should be maintained, so that you
can balance your horse immediately after landing.
This is particularly important when show jumping,
as the fences are fairly close to each other. Chasing
and hunting it is sometimes necessary to let the
reins slip, but they should be shortened up as
quickly as possible.

At the water it is not necessary to start with a
wild hooroosh as is so often seen; this always results
in the horse being unbalanced and sprawling. The
correct procedure is to start at a nice collected pace,
then quicken up from the "slipping point", but
always collected.

Refusal. Now come the important points of
keeping a horse straight and defeating a refusal.

JUMPING

Before reaching this stage the student will of course have a thorough knowledge of the Aids and be able to apply them.

First of all a determined intention on the part of the rider must be in evidence. The slightest sign of nervousness or indecision is quickly conveyed to the horse; this of course is fatal. It makes the nervous horse more nervous. The "not for it" takes full advantage; even the generous jumper begins to have doubts. The Spanish have a proverb: "Fear travels down the reins." How very true.

There are two kinds of refusals: (1) Running out; (2) Stopping dead, and perhaps whipping round.

(1) The horse invariably intimates his intention; it is therefore the rider's business with the help of the Aids, to keep him straight, drive him at it; on arrival at the zone to give him the office, spurs are indicated. But not the whip. Both hands are needed on the reins. If the reins are eased and the spurs applied at the psychological moment, all should be well.

(2) The refuser that stops dead is rather more difficult. The one who tells you he isn't for it, can generally be defeated by determination and a firm giving of the office in no uncertain manner. Should a horse turn round to the left, his hind quarters must swing right. Plenty right leg is required and vice versa. But occasionally one meets a really cunning one, he goes at the fence as if he is going to eat it, then stops dead at the very last moment and perhaps swings round. This customer requires

very determined handling, he must be pushed right into the fence and certainly not be allowed to turn round. At schooling, a man behind with a long whip assists matters considerably with this type.

The main consideration is a really firm seat; the rider who prepares to jump, brings the foot up and swings forward is certain to come unstuck. With a doubtful jumper, it is not safe to swing until you feel that he really means it and is lifting his fore end; it is even better to be late with the swing than to "volunteer" over his head.

Of course it is as well to discover the reason for a horse refusing and have the matter adjusted.

So far we have been dealing with small fences. A sound horse should do quite a lot almost every day, providing the landing is not hard, as part of the usual round, so long as his mouth is not pulled about. It is essential that he be given an immediate award, in the shape of an apple, carrot, cow cake, oats, etc.

The next exercise is to jump fences without wings, which is again simply a matter of the aids and the office. It is a good plan to mark the fence and jump it at that particular spot. When this is accomplished, let two riders come from opposite directions and jump the fence at the same time.

The student should now be qualified to take on fences up to show ring size.

It only now remains to get all the jumping possible, to ride as many different horses as you can. If you have perfected the seat, as I hope I have helped you to do, you will be qualified to hunt in any country and with some schooling to ride chasing and point-to-pointing. I have laid down the general utility seat which I strongly recommend for all purposes.

CHAPTER XI

RIDING A POINT-TO-POINT

THE first essential to riding in a Point-to-Point is to get yourself absolutely fit. Those who haven't been at the game do not realize this dire necessity. To gallop some four miles, sitting absolutely still, to hold your mount well together for say three-quarters of the distance, and, still holding him balanced and nicely together, drive him the rest of the way, requires both wind and strength. But that is only the first step. You must ride as much work as ever you can, and above all ride schooling whenever possible. Now this isn't so easy with only one horse. You must therefore tout round, try for a mount or two in other races, offer to ride exercise, or, as a last resort, hire, and ask for a real puller.

Now comes the day of the meeting. You must walk the course, preferably the day before; and don't be in a hurry. Study the going, the fences, gradients, in fact every point which will help you towards going the shortest way and on the best ground. You ought to be able to make a rough map from memory after your walk round. Walking round in the morning or just before racing starts is invariably too hurried, you will not have time to memorize the course. If you walk round some days beforehand, heavy rain may fall and naturally alter the going.

Know your weight in kit, have your weight cloth packed according to the exact weight you have to carry. Pack as many weights as possible right forward, leaving a couple of pockets empty where your knee goes. Try it on your saddle, and ride a canter just to make sure. The weights must be equally distributed on either side. Have a few spare weights loose in case they may be needed. See that your gear is complete; pay particular attention to the soundness of girths, leathers, reins and surcingle. If you're going to ride in light boots, you may require smaller irons: try them and make sure. Have ordinary goloshes, and slip them off just before you get up, but don't weigh out in them. When packing for the meeting lay everything out, check it over carefully. It is extraordinary the number of men who have to run round the dressing-tent trying to borrow this, that, or the other thing.

Practise getting chucked up. It's easy when you know how, but requires a bit of practice on the part of both the chucker and the chuckee.

It is understood, naturally, that your mount has undergone his preparation, is fit and schooled. If he is running in bandages, see that the tapes have been removed, and that the bandages are sewn on with needle and strong cotton; this is quite easy with one of those curved needles.

Get down to the post neither too soon nor too

late. There's not likely to be a draw for places, so get the inside, you'll be "under the flag". Don't hesitate to say "wait a bit" to the starter if you're not facing right, get your horse well collected and on his toes, keep one eye on the starter and his flag, and get away right in front. If you lose distance at the start, you will have to make it up sometime in the race, and remember that you can give away weight but never distance. It is, of course, presumed that your horse will go in the lead, and has been schooled to gallop his fences; even so, you mustn't bring him to the first fence unbalanced and out of hand, otherwise you may not get much farther.

Over the first fence take a pull and see what is happening. Someone may be taken charge of, let him go. Someone may be settling down in the lead, just going a nice gallop and setting the pace you want. Keep nicely placed, all is well. Maybe no one is pushing on, so go up in the lead, but don't overforce the pace or you'll "cut your horse's throat".

After a few fences you'll know more. Don't go a yard too far, keep on the inside. If a turning flag is set in the fence, pull back a bit, and, if you can do it without pulling across anyone or interfering, jump it a bit sidewise and you'll gain lengths.

Beware of the cunning old bird who is waiting in front, running the race to suit himself. Don't ask for trouble at your fences; if you're not in the front row of the stalls, don't jam yourself right up against those immediately in front of you. Your horse won't get a sight of the fence, will have to jump at short notice, or may blunder right into it. It is fatal to try to shorten your stride when galloping your fences, particularly when close up. When you feel he isn't coming to it absolutely in his stride, or he takes off too soon, leave him to it, go with him, sit tight, don't pull his face, trust in the Lord, and all will be well. When schooling, you must learn to lengthen his stride so as to bring him to his fence just right. There are not so many horses which can always measure their stroke.

If you are upsides with a horse, watch it; an old hand may just accelerate the last stride or two so that as you come to the fence you are half-a-length or so behind. When his horse takes off yours may do likewise, and you're "pipped". Keep one eye on him, the other on the fence; if he moves, go with him.

It is just possible that you may come up against the sort that starts shouting, "Look out, keep straight. Where are you coming to?" with interjected expletives. He's either seeing the "Red Light" or trying to put you off. The correct reply is "Shut up. Keep straight yourself and leave me alone," or words to that effect. If by any chance you do jump sideways and bump anyone, apologize immediately and express genuine regret.

I have never met any rough-and-tumble stuff in Point-to-Points confined to one Hunt or Regiment, but some of the practitioners who used to frequent the more or less open races rode very "keen". So watch your step, and don't place yourself in a "debatable" position.

It is not good to have your nose level with and on "the inside" of another horse's quarters when just about to round a turning flag. I was once caught that way as a callow youth. I went the wrong side of that flag, and had to pull up. Equally it is injudicious to be similarly placed coming to a fence; if the horse in front is close to the wing, and you are somewhat closer, the front horse might possibly incline a trifle to your side, you are either forced out, or what is more unpleasant, over the wing.

All the time you must be thinking: how is your horse going, how much has he got left? What about the others, how are they going? Don't look round, a glance is sufficient to tell you all you want; don't chat, keep all your wind. Your horse must never sprawl, hold him well together. Always steer a dead straight course, don't jump sideways, never alter direction unless you're a good two lengths clear with no chance of interfering. If a gap or weak place has been punched in a fence keep away from it if possible; other horses and riders are apt to make for it and so collide. Moreover, a horse often jumps "slovenly" at a low place. If you carry a whip don't use it coming at a fence.

Now for the last few fences. It's a monkey to a mousetrap your horse is tiring. Hold him well together, push him a bit if need be, but if he is going well up just hold him. If the others quicken you must go with 'em. Suppose your horse has had enough, don't punish him, ease him a bit, but still hold him together, and keep going. I've known horses to fall at the last two fences, so don't give up all hope. The last fence but one is often the critical one, pull him together and drive him at it but don't get him unbalanced. You may have to steady him a trifle then for the last fence, much, of course, depending on the length of the run in. Generally you can make one run of it. So, while never loosing his head, drive him at it and come right away. Don't mind how much you win by, there's no handicapper looking on, and above all things, don't look round.

Take a pull only when you're well past the post. Ride right into the paddock and up to the weighing-in place. It is hoped that you will have practised slipping off correctly, chucking your near side stirrup over, unsaddling properly, sliding your left arm underneath the saddle and weight cloth, and gathering up your breastplate and martingale. If not, go to a race meeting, see how the jockeys do, and copy them. Get into the scales with a most nonchalant air. But for the love of mike, don't weigh in with your whip. When the "all right" is passed along, assume the great-coat and white scarf, not forgetting the goloshes, and stroll out to receive the well-earned congratulations of your friends, and doubtless relax somewhat from the strict training I hope you have undergone. Riding a winner! It's a grand moment, worth all the trouble, self-denial and expense. And anyway, win or lose, if you are fortunate enough to own a good horse that can gallop and jump, if you can do the weight or get down to it, and are not too long in the tooth, most certainly you should get up and ride in your Hunt Point-to-Point, Bona Fide Hunt Steeplechase, or any such contests within a reasonable radius.

CHAPTER XII

CONCLUSION

THE very large attendance at and the intelligence shown in equine events prove that we British are getting Horse-Minded.

Some twenty or thirty years ago, it was not so. True, we had the International Horse Show and several other big shows in which jumping events were prominent, but dressage was never seen. Now, thanks to the Tests at Badminton and elsewhere, one can learn a great deal by watching experts in every branch of equitation. To watch a workman competing in the Dressage Tests, to see the Aids beautifully, but almost imperceptibly, applied, is an education in itself. The most striking lesson to be learned is that horses trained in dressage are better balanced and more able to do what is asked of them, than those not so trained. The moral is that, while it is not necessary for the ordinary rider to work up to the dressage stage, all who ride or wish to ride, must master the Aids and their application and horses and ponies should be properly Aid-trained.

I used to put all my young horses through the school; it improved their balance, jumping and gallop a very great deal. One of my chargers could lead a ride, behave perfectly on parade and at the same time go chasing and win.

But we must not follow blindly what we see in the ring, particularly in the jumping competition. A number of the competitors who get into the money, and even capture a first prize, lie practically along the horse's back, nose in the mane, knees perhaps just touching the saddle, no grip whatever. They can be of no possible assistance to the horse; they win because the horse is perfectly trained. The slightest peck or jar and they shake off; a refusal and they fly. Watch them, and take warning of what not to do.

These days it is difficult for most people to get enough riding to make them really proficient. Unless one owns horses the only thing to do is to go to a really first class riding school either as a student or a working pupil for at least two years. If this is not practicable, week-ends and all holidays should be devoted to equitation.

For chasing and point-to-pointing—there is really no difference nowadays—it is absolutely essential to ride work and be really fit. In the "good old days" we got two and a half months' winter leave. I arranged mine from the 1st January to the 15th March, the whole of which time I spent in Lincolnshire, near the late John Elsey's stables, where I had a horse or two in training. Starting in 1896 I rode work regularly and stipulated that I was to be treated like any of the lads and made to ride anything. We schooled generally twice a week. A good morning was four 2 miles over the steeple-chase course; two 2 miles over hurdles, as well as some work on the flat. Then a quick change and off hunting with that most sporting pack the South-wold. Work on the flat is excellent practice, because you must keep your place in the string and learn to hold some really hard pullers. I was lucky. John Elsey was a splendid fellow, dead straight and a first class trainer. The late Arthur Gordon, who rode for the stable, was a real artist and I learned much from him.

The next thing was to get as much race experience as possible. In those days there was a very large number of meetings all over the country. Nearly every hunt, practically every cavalry regiment, and we (the Gunners) had meetings. Then of course there was the Grand Military Meeting at Sandown. I therefore got what riding I could with my own or friends' horses and picked up what stray mounts were going; though these were not of the best, being out either for a school in public or what the jockeys didn't want. It was splendid experience. My worst day was six rides, one second and two falls; my best was four rides and four wins. Whilst I was a horse gunner at Woolwich I was whip to the drag, played polo, broke and trained young 'uns. As we did quite a lot of serious soldiering, I was kept pretty busy.

By 1899 I had served a pretty hard apprentice-ship, done quite a bit of rough riding and had been promised some really good mounts, but the Boer War broke out and I was abroad for nine years.

Anyone who really wants to get anywhere should learn the hard way; as I did. In my day there was no allowance for beginners; many gentlemen riders were to all intents professionals. It was a pretty rough school, but I enjoyed every moment of it.

The small Hunt Meeting has faded away, replaced by what is called the Point-to-Point. In the 'nineties the point-to-point was invariably four miles. Only three flags were allowed, two for turning points and one for the finish. It was the best fun in the world; the pace was that of a fast hunt. You picked your own line and all the horses *had been regularly and fairly hunted*. Now all that is changed. A point-to-point is in effect a steeplechase, except that, as a rule, the fences are not regulation size. Horses have to be trained. A rider, who wants to get known and be offered mounts, must ride work seriously when and how he can.

In show jumping, exactly the same applies. You must get as much experience as possible in public and ride at all the shows and gymkhanas you can reach. If possible have a knowledgeable friend to watch you and tell you exactly where you have failed or gone wrong. If and when you become really proficient you will be offered mounts, or better still, become attached to a stable.

I think that a good deal more should be done,

particularly to encourage the bona fide amateur and beginners and to keep out the pot hunters. When I ran gymkhanas before the war, in one of them two classes were for ponies of specified heights, to be ridden by boys or girls of specified age; neither pony nor rider to have won a first, second or third jumping prize. Two brothers won each event. A man I knew told me that both boys and ponies had been "in the money", but he would not lodge an objection. So I informed the father that the prizes were being held over pending an inquiry. I later wrote telling him that if he would sign the enclosed certificate to the effect that neither of his sons nor the ponies had ever won, the prizes would be forwarded. He did not reply!

It is most interesting to examine the evolution of the jumping seat, say during the last fifty years. If the old prints are to be relied on—and why shouldn't they—riders did not lean back when taking off; yet in the Military Riding School, we were taught to lean back when coming to the fence and equally to lean back as the horse took off.

Steeplechase jockeys invariably went right back, landing with their heads almost touching the horse's quarters.

I can't help thinking that this seat came in with the park courses. The horses were definitely jumping against the bit. Yet they jumped well nevertheless. But how they pulled! Authoritative books showed photographs of riders, taking off and landing, leaning right back all the time, the horse's mouth open and a tremendous pull on the reins. That was how we were told to do it. We were never asked to jump without reins.

In this country there was practically no show jumping before the Boer War. At the agricultural shows there were jumping classes, but the entries were meagre. Most hunting men did not approve of or support, what they called circus tricks, while many maintained that horses should not be asked to jump in cold blood. At the Dublin Show though, there was always plenty of "leppin'". At the Military Tournament and at regimental sports there was invariably a jumping class, but the standard was not high.

Meanwhile they had been busy on the Continent. Every European country had military schools of equitation. The officers were supplied with good horses and as they did not hunt or play polo, they had plenty of time for show jumping. In Germany, cavalry officers had even to steeplechase. In the United States and Canada likewise, all this was encouraged.

Therefore at the start of this century we were a good long way behind. But we soon began to catch up, despite the fact that our officers had to find their own horses, which they could rarely afford to keep specially for show jumping; and there were only the regimental riding schools. Civilians also began to compete, but the average seat was inclined to be acrobatic. Eventually, the Cavalry School was started at Netheravon and the late General

Sir Noel Birch, then a Major, took over the Riding
House at Woolwich, where he wrought great and
beneficial changes. The riding of the Woolwich
cadets, and throughout the regiment, improved
most noticeably; Major-General Geoffrey White, of
course also then a Major, succeeded Sir Noel and
carried on the good work. When I returned home
in 1909, we were holding our own. After the First
World War, the Royal Artillery Riding House was
moved to Weedon. Hitherto riding masters were
always promoted from the ranks. They were
excellent fellows, but they simply copied their pre-
decessors.

Before I was given my Jacket* in 1897, I was in a
Field Battery at Sheffield. There was no riding
master and my Major put me in riding charge.
A riding master came from Newcastle and put us
through a fortnight's course. He reported to my
Major that I was teaching my classes all wrong. He
would not have it that if you lean back taking off,
you had to hold on to the reins. I brought a good
free-jumping horse into the school; there was a
fence in the middle. I leaned back and dropped my
reins and though I had a grip in those days, I went
clean over backwards! He would not be convinced. He insisted that I had thrown myself off.
My neck was stiff for weeks! My Major said,
"Never mind, just carry on." I have sat forward
ever since.

At Weedon, young subalterns were put through a

* Appointed to the Royal Horse Artillery.

course to qualify them for the post of Equitation Officers.

A little later, Weedon was taken over by the Army. It is now alas, no more. But while it lasted, it did a grand job in the cause of equitation. What a pity that this country cannot have a school of equitation subsidized by the Government as in so many other countries.

Between the wars, show jumping went with a swing; many civilians and a number of girls and ladies were showing the way. We learned much from some of the Continental officers. In spite of the fact that it was all left to private enterprise, we took our full share of cups.

Since the last war, we have done even better; though it really is a cause for shame, that we have to go round with the hat to get funds to enable our jumping team to compete at the Olympic Games.

The ladies now rank equal with the men and not only at show jumping—at which Miss Pat Smythe leads the world—but at dressage as well. At polo, they play in really fast, hard games in first class company, while at point-to-pointing a number of them have better seats over fences than many men.

When I was teaching before the war, I found the girls keener and more anxious to improve than the boys, though a really keen lad, if shown how, is unbeatable. The riding of the younger generation is very much better than it was in my young days, thanks very largely to the pony clubs which are so well worthy of support. What a debt of gratitude is owed to those who so ably run them. But the instructors in many riding schools have still a lot to learn.

To revert to steeplechasing; I am taking a terrible risk in asserting that for a few years before the last war, soldier riders, without a quarter of the practice, were sitting their fences better than the majority of professional jockeys. You need only make a detailed study of the pre-war photographs to see that this is so.

To-day, practically all the professionals sit forward at their fences and go with the horse instead of against him. I think that Tim Hyde was the first to do so. I am quite positive that Workman, good stout horse that he was, owed his success very largely to the masterly way he was ridden at Liverpool. He was brought balanced to every fence and had his stroke measured for him to a nicety.

Hyde told me, "As a result of instructions on equitation, long before becoming a professional jockey, I have endeavoured to keep my knee and lower leg in the galloping position over fences. I had quite a lot of show jumping before starting race riding, and must admit that this experience to a steeplechase jockey is invaluable."

As I have said, we see quite a lot of acrobatic contortionists jumping and even winning in big competitions. But, should the horse refuse, swing round or peck, they "go for six". So take my advice, ignore them and take as your models the photographs of those great masters, reproduced on Plates V and VI.

To Commandant Bizard we owe a great deal; between the wars he showed us the perfect seat over fences. His quiet style and perfect timing made him a tremendous favourite, as evidenced by the reception he always got, win or lose. The soldier grooms thought quite a lot of him; they are pretty keen judges. "Always the same, he is, never blames the horse, the light, the fences or the judges. A real gent and sportsman, not like some of those others," I overheard one say.

It is good to see what a gallant effort is being made to get polo—that game of games—going again in this country, though at the moment, it is mostly kept alive by our marvellous veterans; but alas! there are so few recruits. This may be because the young 'uns have not the time to spare from their work or lack the money to bear the high cost of the game.

There are plenty of young riders, keen and most anxious to play. Perhaps it may be possible to form gymkhana clubs throughout the country, maybe in conjunction with the pony clubs, where station games could be played. There are plenty of likely ponies about. Players with even only one pony can get two chukkers, sometimes three, three times a week; they of course have to sit down and watch, while their pony has a rub down and a breather and wait until he is ready to go into another game.

It is simply a matter of getting together a certain

VI. LE COMMANDANT BIZARD
(*Photographie Hippique de M. Hervé Blanchard, Saumur*)

number of really keen prospective players, finding a
suitable ground and, above all, an old hand to
coach, umpire, organize and run the show.

It is essential that anyone starting polo should
have

(1) A seat independent of the reins.

(2) A sound working knowledge of the Aids and
the "five reins".

And (3) must make a careful study of the rules
and of a really good book on the game.

THE END